UTILITIES REFORM IN EUROPE

UTILITIES REFORM IN EUROPE

DAVID COEN AND MARK THATCHER
EDITORS

Nova Science Publishers, Inc.
Huntington, New York

Senior Editors: Susan Boriotti and Donna Dennis
Coordinating Editor: Tatiana Shohov
Office Manager: Annette Hellinger
Graphics: Wanda Serrano
Book Production: Matthew Kozlowski, Jonathan Rose and Jennifer Vogt
Circulation: Cathy DeGregory, Ave Maria Gonzalez, Ron Hedges and Andre Tillman

Library of Congress Cataloging-in-Publication Data
Available Upon Request

ISBN 1-59033-064-1.

227 Main Street, Suite 100
Huntington, New York 11743
Tele. 631-424-6682 Fax 631-425-5933
E Mail: Novascience@earthlink.net

Printed in the United States of America

CONTENTS

INTRODUCTION: THE REFORM OF UTILITIES REGULATION IN THE EU 1
David Coen and Mark Thatcher
THE NATIONAL POLITICS OF EUROPEAN REGULATION: INSTITUTIONAL REFORM IN TELECOMMUNICATIONS 11
Mark Thatcher
CONFIGURATIONS OF ECONOMIC REGULATION IN THE EUROPEAN UNION: THE CASE OF ELECTRICITY IN COMPARATIVE PERSPECTIVE 31
Burkard Eberlein
THE RISE OF THE COMPETITION STATE: THE DYNAMICS OF BRITISH AND AMERICAN TELECOM AND ELECTRICITY REGIMES 51
David Levi-Faur
DESIGNING ECONOMIC REGULATORY INSTITUTIONS FOR EUROPEAN NETWORK INDUSTRIES 79
David Coen and Chris Doyle
STYLES OF REGULATION: THE CHOICE OF APPROACH TO UTILITY REGULATION IN CENTRAL AND EASTERN EUROPE 101
Jon Stern
INDEX 127

INTRODUCTION: THE REFORM OF UTILITIES REGULATION IN THE EU

David Coen
London Business School
Mark Thatcher
London School of Economics

The creation of the single market and the liberalisation of European utility sectors have resulted in a rapid expansion of EU/EC economic regulation. This has formed part of a wider process of regulatory reform in the sectors at the national and international level. By examining the interaction of economic and political actors in this evolving European market, this special issue addresses some of the questions relating to the appropriate models, institutions and level of regulation. Drawing on comparative sector studies, the papers illustrate how boundaries are shifting through growing liberalisation and consequent internationalization of economic interests. In the course of discussing the above, the papers attempt to assess the degree of European regulatory convergence and address how economic actors play the different tiers of the 'multi-level game'.

Public utilities constitute a large section of Europe's economy. Traditionally, they have been at the heart of national states and their industrial strategies. Moreover, some, such as telecommunications and electricity, are strategic- their supply affects other sectors. At the same time, the sectors are populated by large, powerful suppliers, traditional state-owned organizations, privatized 'national champions' and new entrants, from other sectors and/or abroad. The utilities therefore offer an important case to analyze European regulation, in terms of their own size and weight, their political significance and their past histories.

Liberalisation and the development of supra-national regulation raise economic and social reasons for altering the regulation of public utilities. These include preventing abuse of a dominant position, creating a licensing regime that ensures that competition between firms is fair, protecting social goals such as 'universal service' and seeking to promote appropriate quality information. However, regulatory reform is also a highly political matter, with conflicts and debates over the form of regulatory regime and the substantive content of regulation. Moreover, the extension of EC regulation has resulted in a complex regulatory framework with both national and supra-national competencies.

The papers in this volume examine the political and historical aspects of utilities reform in Europe. They assess the extent and nature of change, the conflicts in reform and the evolving regulatory regime(s). They also address issues of institutional modification and design, including the interplay between different regulators (especially at the EC and national levels). In coming to terms with the above the papers explore four interrelated themes:

1. The characteristics of Europe-wide regulatory reform
2. The nature of national variance under EC's regulatory regime
3. Cross-sectoral variations
4. The institutional arrangements that can develop to accommodate the emerging .

This article introduces the special issue, and attempts to draw out some of the main conclusions and policy implications. We have chosen to address these regulatory questions by drawing on an overview of EC utilities regulation (Coen and Doyle), and comparative case studies of telecommunications and electricity (Thatcher, Eberlein and Levy-Faur). The two utility sectors examined in detail are deemed to warrant regulatory control due to market failure and social considerations. Both sectors have moved from nationalised monopolies in the 1980s to a liberalised market that is increasingly regulated at the European level. Moreover, both sectors under pressure from the ECJ and DGIV, have developed similar economic frameworks and legal EU principles (Pelkmans 1997). Finally, in the late 1990s, the Commission, under pressure from the European Parliament and member states, has accepted the principle of EU "general public services" and utilities (Hancher 1996). Yet, for all the potential convergence, the sectors demonstrate interesting variance in both national and European regulatory institutions and speed at which liberalisation occurs.

1. Europe-Wide Regulatory Reform: Fragmented, Complex and Interacting

The old regulatory regime for European utilities involved certain features that were present in most European nations: public ownership of many utility suppliers; monopoly supply; regulation by government ministries or sub-national government; the absence of general competition law. Regulation was highly national- the EC played almost no role. That regime has steadily been undermined and replaced over the past decade. This can be seen as part of the development of a European 'regulatory state' (Majone 1996, 1997). However, the papers seek to advance the analysis by asking several questions about reform. What does the new regulatory regime look like? What have been the processes of change? What have been the key forces behind reform?

Utilities regulation has seen moves towards liberalisation, accompanied by 're-regulation' of competition, and often privatisation of public sector suppliers. Nevertheless, several elements of the previous regime remain- for example, many suppliers remain publicly-owned (partially or totally) and important areas of supply remain under de jure or de facto monopoly supply. Moreover, no simple regime has entirely replaced the previous one of national regulation and supply by publicly-owned monopolies. Instead, a complex system has emerged that consists of interactions between sets of regulatory institutions, with much over-lay and overlap between them.

The papers analyse the development of multi-level regulation. The most important levels are the national and the EC, although in Germany, the regional level is also significant. The EC has steadily expanded its regulatory regime in the utilities, as Coen and Doyle point out. Yet, as Eberlein and Thatcher also show, this has not meant the end of national regulation. Instead, the EC regulatory regime is incomplete, allows national variation and relies on national regulatory authorities for implementation.

The interplay between sector-specific regulators and general competition authorities offers a second, important aspect of the new regime. At the EC level, this is seen in the involvement of both the competition Directorate General DG IV and more sectorally-based DGs, such as DG XIII for telecommunications. At the national level, there is a mix of general competition law and sector-specific regulation.

The coexistence of principles from several regulatory regimes within the utilities offers another set of interactions. Ideal types offer a useful analytical tool (cf. Levy-Faur), but detailed analysis of sectors indicates that competition sits side by side with continuing 'public service' principles such as universal service and price control.

The processes of change have involved conflict and debate. At the EC level, national governments have not always welcomed the expansion of EC regulation. Within member states, changes such as liberalisation and privatisation have seen vigorous resistance, especially by trade unions and at times, parts of the Left.

Change has been driven by several forces. EC regulation is one: hence while Coen and Doyle analyse the expansion of EC activity, Eberlein and Thatcher assess its impacts. They point out the other factors at work in member states. International developments have been important- for example, technological and economic transformations or reforms in the US (which offer a useful comparison with European regulation). New ideas have emerged concerning liberalisation and privatisation. Domestic interests have altered, resulting in pressures for change or adding strength to pre-existing reform movements. The EC has become a significant force for reform; yet, it is only one influence and at times, it may be less important than other pressures or its role may be mainly legitimise reforms undertaken for other reasons (cf. Thatcher, this volume).

The complex and fragmented nature of the regulatory regime in the utilities leads to three further issues that are addressed by the papers. The first concerns the existence of significant differences among European countries. The second concerns contrasts between utility sectors. The third issue is possible reforms given the complexity of the current regulatory arrangements.

2. National Variation within the EC's Regulatory Regime

he EC's sector-specific regulatory regimes for the utilities during the 1980s and 1990s, particularly for telecoms and electricity have impacted on national regulation, acting as a force for change. Yet 'Europeanisation' has not led to uniformity: regulatory reform and regimes have varied among member states. The papers explore three aspects of cross-national differences.

The first concerns the extent to which cross-national institutional differences have persisted during the 1990s. Eberlein and Thatcher examine continuing contrasts in ownership, regulatory organisation and principles. Thus, for example, whereas almost all suppliers are privately-owned in Britain, majority shares in the incumbent telecommunications operators France Télécom and Deutsche Telekom remain in state hands, whilst the electricity industry in France is still wholly publicly-owned, but in German it is predominantly privately-owned with the state and municipalities holding only small shareholdings. As Eberlein shows, the German electricity sector is also highly fragmented, in stark contrast to France. National regulatory authorities also differ in institutional status: there are sector-specific bodies in Britain, but no such equivalent in German electricity, for example. The principles of regulation also vary: the semi-autonomous regulators in Britain have placed competition at the centre of their concerns (Thatcher 1998), whereas 'public service' has kept a higher profile in France and Germany. Hence there is greater institutional scope for measures to, for instance, protect economically and socially vulnerable groups or promote environmental protection than in Britain. The extent of competition varies markedly across nations, especially in electricity, ranging from competition throughout the entire sector in Britain to continuing dominance in France by one supplier. Differences in the extent of liberalisation result in contrasts in national regulatory activity. The evolution from monopoly to (regulated) competition sees a concomitant move in regulatory activity from preventing abuse of monopoly positions in retail markets to regulation of interconnection and then, as competition becomes self-sustaining, to more 'light-handed' regulation (see Coen and Doyle, this volume).

The path and processes of reform have varied among EC member states, offering a second aspect of the analysis. In both telecoms and electricity (see Thatcher and Eberlein), the timing of change has differed. In Britain, change was introduced from the early 1980s in a politically partisan manner by Conservative Party governments. It was frequently rapid as both sectors were entirely were privatised between 1984 and 1990; other utility sectors underwent a similar process (cf. Hansard Society 1996). Opposition, for example by the trade unions, was speedily overcome, and by 1997, the Labour Party had accepted many of the principles of the new regime, such as private ownership and competition. Moreover, as Levy-Faur argues (this volume), change continued over more than a decade, from the early1980s until the mid-1990s, as Britain moved away through a provisional regimes towards one of ordered competition (cf. also Prosser 1997). Reforms have taken place later in France, Germany and Italy than in Britain, mostly during the mid-1990s. They have involved extensive debates and have met more powerful opposition that has limited or at least held up privatisation and liberalisation. Thus in electricity, the French and German governments had done little to move away from traditional regulatory structures by the mid-1990s, whilst change in telecoms had also occurred later than in Britain.

Given the different regulatory structures in pace, the impact of EC regulation on national regulatory reforms has also differed. Eberlein and Thatcher analyse how EC measures met and interacted with the various national 'landscapes', giving rise to contrasts in impacts. For Britain, the regulatory requirements of EC legislation were negligible, as almost all had already been introduced and the suppliers had been privatised. In contrast, EC requirements posed much greater challenges for other member states. France, Germany and Italy were obliged to allow greater competition; the structure of their industries appeared unsuitable for the new environment, especially when fragmented and/or in traditional public sector institutional arrangements.

Why have such important cross-national variations persisted despite the development of important EC regulatory regimes in the utilities? The papers in this volume point out several factors. First, the EC regime is incomplete and allows much scope for different institutional forms, as well as interpretation and flexibility. Second, as Levy-Faur sets out, there are several competing, although often overlapping, models of regulation. Third, there are different domestic configurations.

The role of domestic politics in explaining cross-national variations is examined in detail in telecoms and electricity by Eberlein and Thatcher, who point to several influences that result in contrasting national paths of regulatory reform. One relates to differences in existing national institutions, both sectoral and more general political institutions. Domestic institutions have provided varied starting points for nations; they have also influenced national capacities for regulatory reform. A second set of factors concerns domestic interests. Party politics have differed among member states; so too has the power of interests such as trade unions. The interests and position of key actors such users, managers of incumbent suppliers and new entrants, especially their degree of dissatisfaction with existing regulatory arrangements and their support for liberalisation and privatisation, have also varied from one member state to another. The ideas of national actors have differed. Despite a degree of cross-national 'policy learning', national traditions concerning matters such as 'service public' and the nature of the 'public interest' have remained resilient and continue to be marked by significant contrasts.

3. Cross-sectoral Variations

Alongside cross-national differences there exist important cross-sectoral ones. The papers highlight contrasts in the EC's regulatory regime, the development of competition, the structure of supply and regulation, and the mix of sector-specific regulation and general competition law.

The extent to which the EC has instituted detailed sector-specific regulatory regimes has differed from one utility to another (for an overview, see Coen and Doyle, this volume; cf. Héritier 1999). Similarly, the timing of EC action has varied. The most detailed and earliest regime came in telecoms (cf. Thatcher, this volume), where EC action began in the late 1980s, so that by the mid-1990s, EC measures affected the entire sector; they both ended national monopolies and provided a comprehensive framework of re-regulation. In electricity, as Eberlein points out, EC action came later and only insisted on partial liberalisation; it also offered many fewer re-regulatory measures. In other sectors, such as gas and postal services, EC regulation has been even later and more limited.

The extent of regulatory reform has also differed among sectors, as is shown by an overview of the various utility sectors (Coen and Doyle) or by comparing the detailed analyses of telecommunications and electricity (Eberlein and Thatcher). In telecommunications, competition has developed in all large EC countries, the organisational status of most public telecommunications operators has been altered (most notably with partial or complete privatisation) and new regulatory bodies have been established. Change has been less marked in other utilities, such as electricity, gas and postal services. Analysis of electricity shows that in most of continental Europe, competition is gradually establishing itself, public and private ownership is mixed and new regulatory bodies either have not yet been established or are much more recent than in telecoms.

The role of EC regulation also shows cross-sectoral contrasts. These can be, however, a little surprising. In telecommunications, Thatcher argues that although the EC has developed a regime covering the entire sector, it only been one factor among several responsible for national reforms. Although it became more important in France, Germany and Italy in the 1990s, he argues that other, non-EC pressures such as technological and economic developments, altered interests and new ideas, were more significant. In electricity, whilst EC regulation has been more recent, Eberlein points out that it carries significant implications for France and Germany and has acted as a catalyst for change.

Several reasons emerge for cross-sectoral differences at the national level. First, international pressures such as technological and economic developments and the expansion of cross-border services, have been greater in certain sectors, especially telecommunications, than in others. Second, the EC's regulatory regime has developed to differing degrees. Third, the domestic policy process has affected change, especially the timing of reform. In particular, telecommunications have seen alteration before other sectors. Hence there has been cross-sectoral learning, leading, for example, British policy makers to break up the industry to attempt to introduce competition whereas BT was the first utility privatisation and was sold as a vertically-integrated virtual monopolist.

4. How can Institutional Arrangements Develop to Accommodate the Existing Regime?

Recognising that the current EU regulatory regime has evolved in an ad-hoc fashion, we explore how member states and firms utilised the multilevel regime for their interests. Nevertheless, we also recognise that if the new liberalised utilities are to continue to operate efficiently and effectively it is important that the EU and member states put effective institutional structures in place. David Levi-Faur develops the normative discussion by exploring ideal types of utility regulation over time and discusses the potential merits of a regulatory regime or a competitive state. At a more practical level, Coen and Doyle's paper explicitly examines the potential regulatory design governing EU utilities, and develops a framework within which key criteria shaping regulatory structures can be compared against 4 potential EU regulatory regimes - Status Quo, Federal Regulation, Regulatory Agency, Regulatory Forum. Accordingly, the paper poses the question of what makes a credible regulatory regime and then assesses credibility and what political price?

In a recent European Commission communication it was asserted that "*NRAs are the rock on which full and uniformed implementation of the regulatory package is built. They need a strongly supportive national framework to enable them to function effectively. This includes providing them with the necessary human and financial resources and the legal and political environment which will enable them to perform their prescribed tasks.*[1]" This assertion, as Thatcher demonstrates for telecommunications, is justified as the national regulatory authorities are close to national markets and perform an essential task in assisting in achieving uniformed implementation of EU directives. Nevertheless, as Eberlein and Coen and Doyle explore, disparities in the powers and resources available and the differences in regulatory procedure undermine their effectiveness. Thus, in accepting the concept of subsidiarity and the continued to delegate decision-making to the NRAs it is clear that any new EU regime must also establish checks and counter balances on NRAs decisions.

A number of regulatory reforms have been put forward in recent years. One possible solution is to centralise the regulatory process by creating a federal regulatory Commission that sets European principles, implementation and enforcement. This would provide independence from member state intervention and a legitimate and clear regulatory procedure. Nevertheless, while favoured by some member states, like Germany and Italy, a new autonomous institution would require significant changes to the treaties and most member states would be reluctant to concede regulatory competencies (Everson 1996). Alternatively, Majone (1997) suggested 'regulation by information' and the creation of specialist European regulatory agencies (Majone 1996, Kreher 1997, Shapiro 1997). Such a regime would set European principles and lead implementation and enforcement by incorporating existing NRAs expertise. It was argued that European agencies by co-ordinating the national regulatory environments,

---

[1] The 1999 Communication Review COM (1999) 539.

would minimise the potential national regulatory "races to the bottom" and create transparent and accountable regulatory institutions (See McGowan and Wallace 1996, Wilks 1996, and Majone 1996). Nevertheless, Coen and Doyle observe that for all the perceived benefits of European agencies, and pressure from the European Parliament, the Commission and member states appear reluctant to hand over executive powers to a new European institution. Instead, there would appear to be a consensus of opinion that would favour the creation of European sector networks of NRAs.

Assuming that these new European regulatory forums would set European principles while allowing the NRAs to lead on implementation and enforcement then it is possible to envisage that these committees and co-ordination networks would gradually encourage procedural convergence and harmonisation of national regulatory experts. However, the opaque nature of many of these committees creates problems of accountability and transparency in the regulatory system and undermines their ability

enforce judgements. Consequently, Coen and Doyle suggest, from a simple cost-benefit study, that regulatory networks represent a second best but credible solution to regulatory agency regimes and federal cartel models.

In sum, we can expect EU institutions to continue to encourage some form of regulatory convergence in member states and for European best practice/principles to gradually evolve for co-ordinated NRAs and NCAs networks. Yet it is also clear that the role of NRAs will continue to be crucial to the success of the internal market and the development of new regulatory regimes. Finally, the papers in this issue would appear to demonstrate the continued multiple speed of harmonisation across sectors and countries and the continued variance in business culture and institutional solutions.

5. Concluding Comments

Accepting that reforms to EU utility policy were technologically and market driven, this issue attempted to address the characteristics of European-wide regulatory reform, and proposed institutional arrangements to accommodate the evolving regime. The research indicated that despite a degree of cross-national 'policy learning', national variance remained and that one EU regulatory model would not be appropriate for all sectors. However, it is equally apparent that EU economic and legal principles have developed and that the current institutional regime must establish clear rules and norms.

Thatcher and Eberlein illustrated that the expansion of EU regulation in the 1990s was closely intertwined with the dynamics of domestic reform in the member states. Moreover, regulation was uneven across sectors and countries and at the mercy of the national institutions and domestic and European interests. Rather, EU regulation was used by reformers and new entrants to reinforce liberalisation and resisted by trade unions and incumbent firms. At a normative level, Levi-Faur observed how new ideas and reforms taken in the US and UK contributed to change at the European regulatory level.

Although competition has been introduced in many regulated utility sectors, the continuation of widespread public ownership and state aid, and political and institutional diversity has called into question the concept of a level EU playing field. The case studies of Thatcher and Eberlein - telecommunications and electricity - illustrated how the current EU regime has evolved in an ad-hoc fashion and presented a number of the opportunities and problems for incumbents, new-entrant firms and national governments. Therefore, Coen and Doyle predicted that a degree of European co-ordination would have to occur if European utility markets were to establish fair competition and international competitiveness. How this co-ordination evolves was harder to assess, but it is fair to say that whether it was a European agency or a network of national regulatory bodies, the regime must provide enough flexibility to allow for national variation and political reservations while maintaining credibility and enforcement powers.

REFERENCES

Bergman, L. Doyle, C. Gual, J. Hultrantz, L. Neven, D. Roller, L. Waverman, L (1998) *Europe's Network Industries: Conflicting Priorities.* Monitoring European Deregulation series 1, London, CEPR.

Hancher, L. (1996) Utilities policy and the European Union, an overview, in: *Regulatory Review* 1996, London CRI.

Hansard Society(1996), *Report of the Commission on the Regulation of the Privatised Utilities* (London: Hansard Society, 1996),

Héritier, Adrienne (1999), *After liberalization: public-interest services in the utilities* (Cambridge: Cambridge University Press)

Everson, M. (1996) The German Federal Supervisory Authority for insurance, in: R*egulating Europe*, London Routledge 1996

Kreher, A. (1997), Agencies in the EC - a step towards administrative integration in Europe, *Journal of European Public Policy*, Vol. 4:2.

Majone, G. (1994), "The rise of the Regulatory State" *West European Politics,* 17:3.

Majone, G. (1996), *Regulating Europe,* London, Routledge.

Majone, G. (1997), The new European agencies: regulation by information, *Journal of European Public Policy Vol. 4.2.*

McGowan, F. and Wallace, H. (1996) "Towards a European Regulatory State" *Journal of European Public Policy*, Vol. 3:4

Prosser, Tony (1997), *Law and the Regulators* (Oxford: Clarendon Press)

Shapiro, M. 1997, the problems of independent agencies in the US and the EU, *Journal of European Public Policy*, Vol. 4:2.

Thatcher, Mark (1998), 'Regulation, Institutions and Change: independent regulatory agencies in the British privatised utilities', *West European Politics,* 21(1): 120-147.

Wilks, S. (1996) "Regulatory Compliance and capitalist diversity in Europe" in *Journal of European Public Policy*, Vol.3:4.

THE NATIONAL POLITICS OF EUROPEAN REGULATION: INSTITUTIONAL REFORM IN TELECOMMUNICATIONS

Mark Thatcher
Department of Government
London School of Economics[1]

Telecommunications has become a core area of integration, as the EC[2] has developed a legally-binding regulatory regime in the 1980s and 1990s. Attention has also been concentrated on analysing the characteristics of EC regulation and the conditions for its development (Natallichi 1999, Sandholtz 1998, Thatcher 1997, Scott and Audéod 1996, Schmidt 1996a, 1997, Sauter 1995, 1997).

Yet focusing entirely at the EC level provides only a very partial view of the role and importance of EC regulation. The strategies of actors at the EC level are often strongly rooted in domestic politics. The EC relies heavily on implementation by member states, notably through alteration of national rules and procedures, and effective action to ensure respect of EC law in practice. Moreover, the importance and novelty of EC regulation must be investigated rather than assumed: at times, it is merely a reflection of existing national regulation; it is one force for change among several, including national and international factors.

The present article looks at the impact of the EC regulatory regime on member states in the case of telecommunications. It focuses on the reform of formal rules and organisational arrangements in member states. These effects provide a good test of the impact of European Community/Union regulation for three major reasons. First, most EC regulation takes the form of formal rules that must then be implemented at national level. Second, national institutions have been claimed to be stable and highly resistant to change, being rooted in differing national histories (Immergut 1992, Hattam 1993, Steinmo 1993, Dobbin 1994, Thatcher 1999b). Third, 'institutionalist' explanations of policy making argue that institutions strongly influence the strategies and roles of actors in national decision making and markets (Hall 1986, Immergut 1992; Weir 1992).

---

[1] The present paper was written during a Jean Monnet Fellowship at the Robert Schuman Centre, European University Institute; the author expresses his gratitude to the Centre and EUI.

[2] The term EC is used as almost all telecommunications regulation has taken place under the European Community pillar of the EU.

Assessing the impact of EC regulation is far from easy, as a single factor must be disentangled from the many influences on institutional reform. Nevertheless, certain questions can be posed to guide analysis:

- To what extent were EC requirements novel for member states? The question allows consideration of whether the EC led change, or whether EC rules were following existing national arrangements.
- What were the forms and mechanisms whereby EC regulation influenced national institutional reform? Hence causal pathways can be analysed.
- What other factors were involved in the modification of institutions in member states and how did EC regulation interact with such them?
- Finally, and most difficult, what was the importance of EC regulation relative to other influences for change?

The impacts of EC regulation on institutional reform are compared across the four largest EC member states: Britain, France, Germany and Italy. Institutional reform was at the centre of policy debates in the sector and change was a visible and contested process. Moreover, the four countries had national differences that permit appreciation of the various mechanisms whereby the EC could affect institutional reform, together with the limits on the EC's roles. More generally, telecommunications have been at the heart of national debates about industrial policy and restructuring the state (V. Schmidt 1996, 2000).

The article therefore begins by briefly setting out the national institutional structures that existed before the mid-1980s in telecommunications and the main pressures for change, before looking at the key features and requirements of EC regulation most relevant to institutional reform (sections I and II); the purpose is not explain the development of national institutional arrangements or EC regulation, but to set them out in order to allow analysis of the impact of the latter on the former. The article then compares alteration of two key institutional arrangements: liberalisation and regulation of competition; organisational structures, including ownership and regulatory bodies and power (sections III and IV). The concluding section seeks to link the findings to more general arguments about the impacts of EC regulation and the factors that influence those impacts.

I. The Terrain for EC Action: National Institutional Structures by the Mid 1980s and Pressures for Change

Many formal institutional features of telecommunications were similar in Britain, France, Germany and Italy before the 1980s (Foreman-Peck and Müller 1988). They were also long-standing, dating from the early part of the century. Publicly-owned PTOs (public telecommunications operators) held monopolies over the building and operation of public telecommunications networks and the supply of almost all telecommunications services and customer premises equipment. The PTOs were:

- the Post Office in Britain;
- the DGT (Direction générale des télécommunications) in France;
- the Deutsches Bundespost in West Germany;
- Italy differed somewhat in having fragmented supply, with several publicly-owned PTOs; the largest PTO was the ASST (l'Azienda di Stato per i Servici Telefonica).

Most PTOs formed part of the civil service and were linked to postal services, being units within PTT (Post, Telegraph and Telephone) ministries;[3] Britain after 1969 was an exception, as the Post Office ceased to be a government department and became a public corporation, with its own legal identity. Users had almost no legal rights and there were no independent regulators for telecommunications: the PTT Ministries combined the functions of suppliers, national regulators and policy makers. Indeed, the concept of 'regulation' was rarely applied to telecommunications in Western Europe.

The traditional institutional frameworks in the four countries faced increasing transnational and domestic pressures for change from the late 1960s onwards. Technological and economic developments, notably the application of computing to telecommunications, transformed the sector: they undermined monopolies by making entry and competition viable; they contributed to increased and more diverse demand, increasing pressure for liberalisation and moves away from the old departmental, postal model of supply (Stehman 1995; Thatcher 1999b; Vickers and Yarrow 1988). Reforms in the United States offered an example of reform and also triggered lobbying by American policy makers and suppliers; in particular, liberalisation of services and CPE and the breakup of AT&T in 1984 led to challenges to national monopolies in Europe (Hills 1986). New ideas emerged, particularly in the United States, concerning the benefits of competition (Baumol et al 1982; Stigler 1971, Peltzman 1976, Kolko 1977). A fourth factor for change was the development of EC regulation.

II. Institutional Aspects of EC Regulation

Until the mid-1980s, the EC played almost no role in the regulation of telecommunications. The mid-1980s saw the beginnings of EC action, leading to a Green Paper in 1987 (CEC 1987). Thereafter, an increasingly rapid flow of regulatory measures (Directives and Decisions) ensued (Thatcher 1997; Sauter 1995, 1997 ch5; Scott and Audéoud 1996). Most concerned competition and required implementation through formal rules and organisational arrangements. They comprised three types of provisions: liberalisation measures; re-regulatory rules; a few requirements concerning the structure of regulatory bodies.

Liberalisation took the form of prohibitions on member states from maintaining legal monopolies over supply ('special and exclusive rights'). Initially, it was confined to limited segments of the telecommunications market. The main legislation was:

- the Terminals Directive of 1988 (CEC 1988) permitted competition in the supply of all types of customer premises equipment;
- the 1990 Services Directive (CEC 1990) ended special and exclusive rights over the supply of all telecommunications services, other than 'reserved services' (voice telephony and telex services);
- the 1994 Satellites Directive (CEC 1994) insisted that competition be permitted in satellite services and equipment;
- the Mobile Communications Directive (CEC 1996) laid down that competition in mobile services (such as telephony and paging) should be maximised (subject to bandwidth availability) with at least two suppliers being licensed.

These segments were growing very rapidly in all four countries from the late 1980s onwards. Nevertheless, the core of telecommunications remained 'network operation'- fixed-line voice telephony and transmission- which accounted for over 85% of telecommunications revenues. Only in the mid-1990s was liberalisation extended to network operation: in 1995, a Commission Directive allowed cable networks (notably cable television networks) to be used for transmission of all services already opened to competition (CEC 1995); in 1996, a Directive imposed the duty on most member states to allow competition in public fixed-line voice telephony and over the fixed-line infrastructure from 1st January 1998 (CEC 1996).[4] Thus by 1998, the EC regulation banned national monopolies throughout the entire telecommunications sector.

'Re-regulatory' requirements were designed to ensure that 'fair and effective' competition developed. Key conditions of supply for services were laid down in the Open Network Directive (Council 1990), such as non-discrimination, access to networks and cost-oriented tariffs. Other Directives followed that covered issues central to competition throughout the sector: licensing, interconnection and universal service (EP and Council 1997a, 1997b). They prohibited restrictions on the number of new licences except in specified circumstances, insisted that PTOs should negotiate interconnection with each other on a non-discriminatory basis and imposed duties on PTOs with 'significant market power' (for instance, publication of reference tariffs, cost-oriented tariffs and transparent accounting systems).

EC legislation laid down a few stipulations concerning the institutional position of NRAs ('national regulatory authorities'- ie. those bodies responsible for regulation in member states). The most important was that supply and regulation had to be undertaken by legally separated organisations. However, there was no requirements that NRAs be independent of national governments- indeed, PTT ministries were generally counted as

[3] Or Ministries incorporating them; for ease of reference, they are referred to as PTT Ministries.

[4] There were temporary derogations for member states with small or underdeveloped networks; these did not include the four countries studied here.

NRAs. Moreover, EC measures made no almost mention of ownership, since under Article 222 of the Treaty of Rome, the EC cannot intervene in questions of ownership in member states.

III. The Impacts of EC Regulation on Liberalisation and The Regulation of Competition in Member States

The traditional institutional framework in Britain, France, Germany and Italy involved extensive monopolies. Therefore EC legislation giving rights to compete and establishing rules for the operation of competition might appear to have represented a considerable change. Close analysis, however, indicates a complex pattern: EC regulation interacted with other factors operating within the four countries; its impact varied over time; its effects also differed between Britain, where its institutional impact was negligible, and the other three countries.

In the 1980s and early 1990s, EC directives insisting on competition in terminal equipment, and advanced services were largely following reforms rather than leading them: many EC measures had already been introduced or were underway in the four countries. Thus in Britain, BT's monopoly over terminal equipment, 'value-added services' and mobile communications services had been ended in the early 1980s. Similarly, in France and Germany, PTO monopolies over the supply of customer premises equipment and value-added network services had been restricted during the 1980s, and liberalisation in mobile services began in the late 1980s and early 1990s (Schmidt 1991, Thatcher 1999b, Noam 1992). EC regulation was not a new departure; rather, it extended the scope of liberalisation and offered refinements to national rules (Thatcher 1995a, 1996; cf. Schneider et al 1994). The EC's greatest impact was on Italy, where the development of competition was slow, EC Directives required alteration of Italian law and the Commission intervened directly to exert significant pressure for liberalisation (notably for mobile telephony and closed user networks- Il Sole 24 Ore 12.1.95, 20.1.95, 29.3.95, 18.7.95, 4.10.95, 7.6.96 and Stehmann 1995); even so, modest liberalisation was already beginning in the early 1990s at the same time as EC legislation was being passed (Foreman-Peck and Manning 1988, Noam 1992).

Ending PTO monopolies over terminal equipment and advanced services in the four countries were largely driven by non-EC national and transnational factors. One was pressure by large business users who were dependent on high quality advanced telecommunications services and who were dissatisfied with existing PTO supply and restrictions on entry (Cawson et al. 1990; Financial Times 15.4.80, 24.4.81 and 1.10.82, Jäger 1994, Richeri 1985, Foreman-Peck and Manning 1988). Multi-nationals pressed for liberalisation of advanced services and CPE, notably in Germany, where calls for liberalisation were led by IBM, supported by the American government (Schmidt 1991; Financial Times 31.7.86 and 2.6.86). Excess demand played a central role in the liberalisation of mobile networks in all four countries. Perhaps most important of all, it became increasingly difficult in practice to police and enforce restrictions on CPE and advanced services. In the face of these pressures, policy makers gradually accepted liberalisation; change came earliest in Britain, where the Conservative government and especially Oftel pursued an active policy in favour of competition (Thatcher 1994).

Liberalisation of the supply of advanced services and terminal equipment aroused limited controversy: they represented only 10-15% of markets and were not seen as natural monopolies. Much more difficult was allowing competition in network operation- public voice telephony and the building and operation of networks- which constituted the core of telecommunications and accounted for over 85% of sectoral revenues. When EC legislation on competition in voice telephony and the operation of networks was passed in 1995-96, the regulatory adaptation required in Britain differed from that of France, Germany and Italy. Britain had already introduced competition into network operation before EC legislation. Hence EC regulation required little institutional adjustment.

In contrast, France, Germany and Italy still maintained monopolies for their historic PTOs in network operation, and indeed during the 1980s, had made considerable efforts to protect those monopolies. In the early/mid- 1990s, liberalisation often met strong opposition, led by trade unions representing PTO employees and parts of the political left. Moreover, the 're-regulatory' elements of EC legislation were largely new: because of monopoly provision by a state-owned operator, previously there had been few formal requirements over matters such as interconnection, licensing and universal service.

Given the regulatory position France, Germany and Italy, EC regulation of competition in network operation had direct and indirect impacts. EC requirements provided political impetus to overcome inertia and indeed active resistance to liberalisation. Thus, for example, legislation in Germany in 1989-90 and 1994 (Postreforms II and III) extending competition was presented as being necessary to meet EC obligations, in the face of powerful lobbying by the DPG trade union; similarly, in Italy, liberalisation in the mid-1990s followed the requirements of EC law, direct pressure by the EC Commission and the use of EC law by the Anti-Trust Authority (Werle 1999; Natalicchi, 1999; Il Sole 24 Ore 6.2.95, 29.3.95, 18.7.95, 7.6.96, 11.9.96). Later in the 1990s, in order to comply with EC legal requirements to end remaining monopolies, France, Germany and Italy passed major pieces of legislation,[5] together with secondary legislation. The new laws ended monopolies and laid down rules for the regulation of competition, including matters such as interconnection, universal service and licensing; frequently their provisions were explicitly based on EC legislation.

However, EC requirements were not the sole factor behind liberalisation; rather, they formed part of reform debates that emerged in the 1990s in France, Germany and Italy (cf. Bancel-Charensol 1996, Werle 1999). National governments and PTO managements gradually and reluctantly accepted during the 1990s that competition in voice telephony and telecommunications infrastructure provision was inevitable and indeed even beneficial. New ideas, technological and economic changes, privatisation and internationalisation played important parts in this, in addition to EC regulation.

---

[5] In France, the 1996 law on liberalisation and competition, no.96-559; in Germany, the 1996 Telekommunikationsgesetz ('Postreform III'); in Italy, the law no. 249 of 31 July 1997; in Britain, minor modifications were required to meet some EC 're-regulatory' requirements- cf. Hunt 1997.

PTO monopolies over voice telephony and the infrastructure appeared to be increasingly difficult or costly to sustain given developing technologies. PTOs faced the development of 'bypass' (for instance, call-back services or relocation of call centres to lower-cost PTOs) as other countries liberalised and attracted telecommunications-based firms. There was growing pressure for liberalisation by business users, especially large multi-nationals and particularly when monopoly PTOs could not expand supply sufficiently rapidly. Hence, for example, in Germany, there were strong pressures for liberalisation of infrastructures after reunification, as Telekom could not satisfy demand (Robischon 1999; cf. Stehmann 1995, pp.219-221). Politically powerful companies which wished to enter the expanding telecoms market also lobbied governments for change.[6]

New ideas about natural monopoly and the benefits of competition spread. There were claims that countries which maintained restrictions would be left behind other countries which had liberalised: the success of rapid development of advanced telecommunications/information communications services and networks in Britain and the US was linked to liberalisation of their telecommunications markets, increasing the mimetic pressures on other European countries. At the same time, liberalisation in the two countries showed that incumbent PTOs could even thrive in a liberalised market. Britain was seen as a dangerous competitor within Europe, thanks to liberalisation, the presence of the privately-owned BT and its policy of attracting large multi-national telecommunications users (cf. Dandelot 1993, Larcher 1993, Il Sole 24 Ore 6.6.94, 11.5.96, 17.12.96).

Competition was also intimately linked to privatisation and internationalisation, which were vigourously pursued by France Télécom and Deutsche Telekom with the active involvement of their national governments (cf. Cowhey and Aronson 1993). Liberalisation was the quid pro quo of privatisation, which was strongly desired by PTO managements and governments (see section IV): competition was claimed to prevent privately-owned incumbent PTOs exploiting their positions. Liberalisation aided internationalisation: it justified alliances with foreign operators by national PTOs, traditionally symbols of national sovereignty; a single European market offered greater opportunities for cross-national links for PTOs. Moreover, reforms in the United States (notably the ending of AT&T's monopolies and then its break up in 1984) was followed by direct pressure from US companies such as AT&T, Regional Bell Operating Companies and IBM, and from American policy makers, on European policy makers to open up their markets (Cowhey and Aronson 1993, p.281 and Mouline 1996, Vogel 1996, pp.35-38). Yet the American reforms also appeared to offer opportunities for foreign suppliers, including European ones, to enter the largest market in the world. The role of the US was seen most clearly when the acquisition of shareholdings in US operators were made dependent by US regulators on ending monopolies in Europe. In particular, BT's attempts at expansion through its alliance with MCI and the stake taken by France Télécom and Deutsche Telekom in the American operator Sprint, were made

[6] For example, CGE in France, Veba and Mannesman in Germany, and Olivetti, Fiat and Mediaset (owned by Silvio Berusconi) in Italy.

dependent on liberalisation of their home markets by US regulatory authorities (La Tribune Desfossés 15.6.94, 4.12.95, Frankfürter Allgemeiner 24.4.95; Wirtschaftswoche 4.5.95).

Thus liberalisation in EC member states was the product of several factors. The EC's regulatory regime aided the extension of competition in France, Germany and Italy, but it was an additional factor, combining with new ideas, technological and economic pressures and internationalisation.

IV. EC REGULATION AND THE ORGANISATION OF THE STATE

The 1980s and especially the 1990s saw a comprehensive reshaping of state structures in Britain, France, Germany and Italy. In all four countries, changes involved a two-step process away from the traditional structure of the state as regulator, policy maker and supplier. The first stage in reform was that the PTOs (public telecommunications operators) were transformed into autonomous publicly-owned corporations (or their equivalents), with their own legal identity and separated from postal services; the PTT Ministry was left as the main sectoral regulator. The PTOs and the date of their creation were:

- British Telecom, 1981;
- France Télécom, 1990;
- Telekom, 1989-90;
- in Italy, the largest supplier, ASST, was removed from the PTT Ministry in 1992 and the various PTOs consolidated as Telecom Italia in 1994-96.

Thereafter, the PTOs were wholly or partially privatised. Hence 50.1% of shares were sold in BT in 1984, with the remainder being disposed of by 1993. A minority of shares in Deutsche Telekom (DT) and France Télécom were sold in 1996-98, whilst a majority of Telecom Italia shares were sold in 1997. New regulatory authorities were created that were semi-independent from elected politicians:

- Oftel (the Office of Telecommunications);
- the ART (Autorité de régulation des télécommunications);
- the Reguliersungsbehörde in Germany;
- the Autorità for Telecommunications and Broadcasting in Italy.

EC legislation contained few requirements concerning the organisation of the state and did not require privatisation or the creation of semi-autonomous regulators. Nevertheless, in France, Germany and Italy, the EC played an important role in the reform process in the late 1980s and the 1990s: it increased pressures by PTOs managements for new organisational arrangements; it encouraged governments to introduce change; it weakened opponents of institutional modification.

PTO managements in France, Germany and Italy argued that EC liberalisation made reform urgent and indispensable. They claimed that they needed to adjust to a competitive market and that public sector ownership, especially within the civil service, inhibited them from competing effectively with privately-owned giants such as BT and AT&T, because they faced constraints concerning staffing, contracts and expenditure (Roulet, 1994, Le Monde, 6.7.93, 16.7.93; Chevallier, 1996, Schmidt 1996b; Larcher 1996, Le Monde 7.6.97, Il Sole 24 Ore 6.6.94, 29.6.95, 5.8.95, 11.5.96, 6.6.96, 15.2.97). Brandishing the date of 1 January 1998 (the EC deadline for full competition), PTO managements pressed hard for reforms, lobbying governments and mounting public campaigns. Thus, for example, the new head of France Télécom insisted that a new law implementing EC competition provisions in network operation be accompanied by organisational changes for France Télécom and resigned when he failed to receive guarantees of this (Le Monde 10-11.9.95). Similar pressures, utilising the 'threat' posed by full competition were exerted in Germany by Deutsche Telekom and by reformers in Italy (Die Zeit 4.12.92, Financial Times 11.3.93, 26.10.93; Il Sole 24 Ore 29.6.95, 6.12.96, 15.2.97 and 17.3.97).

EC regulation also contributed to decisions by governments in France, Germany and Italy to introduce reforms despite opposition and controversy. On the one hand, the EC could be used to justify reforms. Its regulatory regime, centred on 'fair and effective competition', undermined traditional justifications for public sector supply, such as 'service public' and cross-subsidisation of services and users. Its prohibitions on PTOs continuing their regulatory functions were used to explain the transformation of PTOs into corporations, legally separated from PTT Ministries (Cf. Prévot 1989, pp.133-136, Le Monde 13.10.90 and 6.7.93; Schmidt, 1991). In Italy the Commission even intervened directly: the privatisation of Telecom Italia was linked to the 1993 agreement between the Italian government and competition Commissioner Karel van Miert on state aids (Il Sole 24 Ore 3.3.95, 7.6.96, 11.9.96). On the other hand, governments faced pressures for change not only from their national champion PTOs, but also from competitors to PTOs, who, armed with EC rights, took action to obtain 'fair' treatment. As a result, continued direct regulation of telecommunications became a legally and politically contentious area. Governments faced sharp conflicts between protecting their PTOs and their legal obligations under EC law concerning competition. Telecommunications regulation thus began to offer potentially damaging controversies. The clearest cases arose in Italy, where governments found themselves embroiled in lengthy disputes, caught between Telecom Italia, the Italian Anti-Trust Authority, the EU Commission (particular its powerful competition Directorate, DG IV) and large, influential new entrants such as Olivetti and Fiat.

National coalitions supporting traditional state structures found themselves placed in a defensive position by the EC regulatory regime and struggling against a gradual set of changes that undermined their strength. Their core members were PTO trade unions and employees, who wished to protect the status of employees, and nationalistic supporters of public ownership (traditionally present in parties of both the political left and right) who argued that states should conserve vital areas of economic life under their direct control and prevent private monopolies from exploiting users (Werle 1999; Foreman-Peck and

Manning 1988; Richeri 1985; Cohen 1992; Thatcher 1999b). However, in the face of EC liberalisation, the nationalist wing of the coalition shrank, as competition and regulation rendered public ownership unnecessary to prevent monopoly exploitation of users by private suppliers; reforms were needed for national champion PTOs to survive and prosper. Moreover, EC 'imposed' competition offered a convenient argument for governments of the left faced with opposition from within their parties and coalitions. Thus in France, Germany and Italy, political parties that had hitherto opposed reforms, supported and often introduced them (for example, the French Socialist and Communist parties after 1997 or the former Italian Communist party). Trade unions and employees were left isolated, appearing to cling to outdated structures in pursuit of narrow sectional interests; in the face of EC regulation based on competitive markets, their stance threatened to leave unreformed 'national champion' PTOs vulnerable.

Nevertheless, whilst EC regulation aided reformers and increased incentives for institutional modifications, it was an influence additional to other factors: its role in national politics was to accelerate and facilitate strategies driven by non-EC developments. The process of reform had begun at the national level during the 1980s, as PTO managements and national governments sought to adapt to new conditions. Britain represented an extreme case: BT was privatised and Oftel created in 1984, without reference to the EC. In France and Germany, attempts to move away from civil service status for PTOs were long-standing, dating from the 1960s and 1970s. Then in the mid/late 1980s, the reform movement was revived in earnest, just as the EC began to develop its regulatory framework. Thus in France, the Rocard government established a special commission in 1988 to examine alteration of France Télécom's organisational position, which led to legislation in 1990 that transformed the operator into a form of public corporation (Prévot 1989, Thatcher 1995b, Gensollen 1991). In Germany, the process of reform also got underway through the Witte Commission which was established in 1985 and proposed in 1987 that the Deutsches Bundespost be split into three public corporations, one being Telekom (RegierungsKommission Fernmeldewesen 1987, Werle 1990). In Italy, there had been extensive discussion of reorganisation, although little action was taken because weak governments failed to overcome opposition from political parties and trade unions (Foreman-Peck and Manning 1988; Richeri 1985).

During the 1990s the process of institutional modification accelerated in France, Germany and Italy, due to both EC regulation and non-EC factors. Rather than representing a decisive break or central pressure for change, the EC regulatory regime largely represented a factor congruent with other forces, as reforms were selected and supported by PTO managements and governments for non-EC reasons.

Central in reforms were financial pressures constraints that were often unrelated to the EC's regulatory regime in telecommunications. For governments, privatisation of PTOs offered vital fiscal receipts to reduce debt; in addition, in Germany and Italy, it avoided use of public funds for essential telecommunications investment. For their part, PTO managements had become increasingly resentful during the 1980s and 1990s at their continuing use as instruments of fiscal and industrial policy- for instance, providing payments to the general budget, covering the losses of postal services and offering secure employment Cohen 1992, Thatcher 1999b, Koebberling 1993, pp.55-57, Il Sole 24 Ore

25.6.95; personal interviews). They therefore pressed hard for a new settlement that would free them of such burdens.

The changing demands of telecommunications markets offered another set of pressures for structural reform. Large-scale investment was needed to support advanced services and meet new entrants. Capital requirements were particularly important in Germany, where, following reunification, the costs of modernisation in the former East Germany were very high:[7] privatisation offered the prospect of easier access to capital markets. In Italy, reform was useful because the network needed heavy investment for modernisation. Moreover, PTOs sought to escape the constraints of the public sector in order to adapt to competition that was developing irrespective of EC regulation in fast-growing services (such as mobile telephony and advanced services mixing telecommunications and computing) (see section III). Thus, for example, one of the experiences that impelled Deutsche Telekom to press for privatisation was competition in mobile telephony: following a German government decision to license a second operator (Mannesmann), it found itself outclassed by the newcomer.

Internationalisation was often a key justification for privatisation. PTOs in France, Germany and Italy sought to internationalise, in order to enter the American market and to offer 'global networks and services', especially to multinationals and to match rival PTOs throughout the world, who were forming alliances (Elixmann and Herman 1996; Cowhey and Aronson, 1993, pp.191-6). Governments wished to protect their own 'national champion' PTOs, and hence supported changes that aided PTO internationalisation. However, alliances appeared to require privatisation; public ownership prevented cross-share holdings, made it difficult to value the operators and left PTOs vulnerable to 'political influence' (Roulet 1994, Dandelot 1994, Larcher 1993 and 1996). At times, internationalisation involved very direct linkages to institutional change. Thus, in forming the alliance between France Télécom and Deutsche Telekom, German policy makers urged privatisation of the former.[8] Obtaining regulatory approval by US authorities for an alliance by the two operators with the American operator Sprint became enmeshed in France Télécom's privatisation (Le Monde 3.8.94, 22.7.95).

Ideas about how 'public interests' should be protected and the appropriate role of government also altered in the four countries. Telecommunications formed part of the international wave of attacks on state ownership in the 1980s and 1990s (Feigenbaum, Henig and Hamnett 1998; Ikenberry 1990; Wright 1994). Cross-national policy learning and emulation were important in France, Germany and Italy: the privatisation of BT and the establishment of Oftel in Britain were used as examples of change. Governments saw increasing disadvantages in existing structures and set of relationships as they faced conflicting claims and interests. The increasingly important and demanding large users needed to be satisfied, notably through tariff rebalancing, to increase access and local call charges and reduce long-distance tariffs, a move that threatened to be unpopular with

[7] An estimated DM60billion was required between 1990 and 1997; by 1992, Telekom faced debts of DM100 billion, and debt servicing costs represented 12% of its income of DM 54 billion- The Economist 30.10.93.

[8] Gunter Rexrodt, German Finance Minister even made public comments on the matter- La Tribune Desfossés 18.7.5 and Le Monde 22.7.95.

voters who, as domestic consumers, often lost out. Privatisation and a more distant relation between governments and suppliers, mediated by a semi-independent regulator, allowed elected politicians to avoid or deflect pressures that were increasingly difficult to manage successfully.

Thus whilst the EC's regulatory framework provided reasons for change, other forces were more and direct and powerful in altering the structure of regulation and supply. The EC offered an additional factor; its main role was indirect, namely altering competitive pressures, and as a external justification for reform.

V. Conclusion

The importance and impacts of EC regulation grew over time. By the mid-1990s, the EC's regulatory regime covered the core of the telecommunications sector and contributed to considerable institutional alterations in France, Germany and Italy. It did so through its legal requirements that required the three countries to modify their rules governing competition. Appreciation of the role of the EC, however, must extend further than its legal requirements: the 1990s saw considerable indirect effects, as the logic of EC rules undermined existing arrangements and aided changes that went far beyond the requirements of EC legislation, notably privatisation and the creation of semi-independent regulatory bodies. It strengthened the position of reformers in the three countries by offering them additional arguments to justify changes and aided the broadening of their coalitions as PTO managements, governments and political parties increasingly supported reform. On the other hand, EC regulation weakened the position of opponents of new forms of supply and regulation. Their previous coalitions were reduced, as nationalistic supporters and political parties abandoned them.

Although EC regulation became a significant factor in institutional reform, especially in the 1990s, analysis of national decision making institutional reform reveals that EC measures formed part of broader processes of telecommunications reform within member states. Attempts at reorganising telecommunications had begun in the 1960s and were underway by the 1980s, when EC regulation began. Several of the EC's measures had been already implemented by member states. The most pronounced example was Britain, where EC decisions in the 1980s and 1990s required almost no domestic alterations. However, in France and Germany, most of the EC's legislation during the 1980s, such as liberalisation of terminal and advanced services supply, had also been introduced. Thus in the 1980s, and with respect to Britain in the 1990s as well, EC regulation was following behind domestic action.

Moreover, the expansion of EC regulation in the 1990s was closely intertwined with the dynamics of domestic reform in France, Germany and Italy. National modifications were driven by several host of factors, of which the EC was only one. PTO managements and governments increasingly favoured liberalisation and reorganisation of PTOs in order to adapt to changing conditions, including technological and economic developments, increasing conflicts for national governments between their roles as regulators and owners of suppliers, pressure by users and new entrants and the desire for PTOs to internationalise. New ideas and reforms undertaken in the US and Britain provided further pressures for change. Thus close inspection of domestic politics indicates the importance of non-EC influences in the shifting strategies of national policy makers.

Telecommunications shows that analysis of the role of EC regulation requires an understanding of its interaction with other forces for change operating within member states (cf. Héritier, Knill and Mingers 1996). EC decisions were used by actors at the national level to pursue strategies that were in large measure responses to non-EC factors. The role of the EC's regulatory regime was therefore to reinforce and accelerate moves towards liberalisation and public sector restructuring and to assist reformers in PTOs and national governments in pursuing their strategies of adaptation to new conditions. The force of EC regulation lay in its compatibility with these other factors.

Thus in large measure, the importance of EC regulation was that it joined other pressures for reform. It role was to advantage certain types of actor in the institutional reform process (PTO managements and governments), as they were able to utilise EC regulation for their strategies, and to disadvantage opponents of changre (notably trade unions). The 'two-level game' (cf Putnam 1988, Evans et al 1993) or 'multi-level governance' (cf. Marks 1993, 1997, Hooghe 1996, Marks et al 1996) of EC regulation was therefore not neutral, but contributed to altering the distribution of power at the domestic level. However, this position also meant that EC regulation was one factor amongst several responsible for institutional reform. Moreover, its impacts varied among countries, depending on their existing institutional position; hence not only is EC regulation a 'patchwork' (Héritier 1996), but so are its impacts. Thus, EC regulation must be considered in its context, both national and international: although for analytical purposes it may be useful to separate it out, it is not an isolated influence but forms part of complex processes of change driven by factors operating at national and international levels.

REFERENCES

Bancel-Charensol, L (1996), *La Déréglementation des Télécommunications* (Paris: Economica/ENSPTT).

Bassan, F (1998), 'La Riforma delle telecommunicazione: profili generali', *Diritto del Commercio Internationale* vol 12(1), pp.,3-63.

Baumol, W. J., Panzar, J. and Willig, R. D. (1982), *Contestable Markets and the Theory of Industry Structure* (New York: Harcourt Brace Jovanovich)

Brenac, Edith and Payen, Guy (1988), *Une Politique en Dérive. La DGT et le Plan Câble* (Grenoble: Université de Grenoble).

Cawson, Alan, Holmes, Peter, Webber, Douglas, Morgan, Kevin and Stevens, Ann (1990), *Hostile Brothers* (Oxford: Clarendon Press).

Chevallier, Jacques (1996), 'La nouvelle réforme des télécommunications: ruptures et continuités', *Revue Française de Droit Administratif*, 12(5): 909-51.

CEC-Commission of the European Communities (1987), *Towards a dynamic European economy- Green Paper on the development of the common market for telecommunications services and equipment* (COM(87) 290, 30 June 1987).

CEC-Commission of the European Communities (1988), *Commission directive on competition in the markets in telecommunications terminal equipment*, Commission Directive 88/301/EEC, OJ L 131, 27.5.88.

CEC-Commission of the European Communities (1990), *Commission directive on competition in the markets for telecommunications services*, Commission Directive 90/388/EEC, OJ L 1922, 24.7.90.

CEC-Commission of the European Communities (1994), *Commission Directive 94/46/EC of 13 October 1994 amending Directive 88/301/EEC and Directive 90/388/EEC in particular with regard to satellite communications* (OJ L268/15).

CEC-Commission of the European Communities (1995), *Commission Directive of 18 October 1995 amending Directive 90/388/EEC with regard to the abolition of the restrictions on the use of cable television networks for the provision of already liberalised telecommunications networks*, Directive 95/51/EC (OJ L 256/49, 26.10.95).

CEC-Commission of the European Communities (1996a), *Commission Directive 96/2/EC of 16 January 1996 amending Directive 90/388/EEC with regard to mobile and personal communications* OJ 1996 L20/59).

CEC-Commission of the European Communities (1996b), *Commission Directive of 28 February 1996 amending Directive 90/388/EEC regarding the implementation of full competition in telecommunications markets*, Directive 96/19/EC (OJ L 74/13, 22.3.96).

Cohen, Elie (1992), *Le colbertisme "high tech"* (Paris: Hachette).

Corn, A, Portarollo, E and Preisel, B (1995), The Influence of Community Regulation on National Regulation in Telecommunications Markets, *Revista internationale di scienzi sociale*, 103(1): 183-208.

Costa, A, Pontarollo, E and Preisel, B (1995), 'The influence of Community regulation on National regulation in Telecommunications Markets', *Revista internationale di scienzi socialie*, no103(1), pp183-208

Council of the European Communities, *Council Directive of 28 June 1990 on the establishment of the internal market for telecommunications services through the implementation of open network provision* (90/387/EEC OJ L 192/1, 24.07.90).

Council of the European Communities (1992), *Council Directive of 5 June 1992 on the application of ONP to leased lines* (92/44/EEC OJ L 165/27, 19.06.92).

Council of the European Communities (1995), *Directive of 13 December 1995 on the application of open network provision (ONP) to voice telephony*, Directive 95/62/EC (OJ L321/6, 30.12.95).

Cowhey Peter F and Aronson, Jonathon D (1993), *Managing the World Economy. The consequences of Corporate Alliances* (New York: Council of Foreign Relations)

Cozzi, G and Morganti, F (1995), 'La Regolazione neele telecommunicazioni in Italia', *Economica e politica industriale*, no87, pp53-68.

DGPT (Direction Générale des Postes et Télécommunications) (1994), *Quelle réglementation pour les télécommunications françaises?* (Paris: Ministère de l'Industrie, des Postes et des Télécommunications et du Commerce Extérieur).

Dandelot, Marc (1993), *Le secteur des Télécommunications en France: Rapport au Ministre de l'Industrie, des Postes et Télécommunications et du Commerce Extérieur*, (Paris: PTT Ministry).

Dobbin, Frank (1994), *Forging industrial policy. The United States, Britain, and France in the railway age* (Cambridge: Cambridge University Press).

Dyson, Kenneth and Humphreys, Peter (1990), 'Introduction: politics, markets and communications policies' in Dyson, Kenneth and Humphreys, Peter, (eds), *The Political Economy of Telecommunications* (London and New York: Routledge).

Elixmann, Dieter and Hermann, Herman (1996), 'Strategic Alliances in the Telecommunications Service Sector: Challenges for Corporate Strategy', *Communications & Stratégies*, 24: 57-88.

European Parliament [EP] and Council (1997a), *Directive 97/13/EC on a common framework for general authorizations and individual licences in the field of telecommunications services* (OJ L 117/15, 7.5.97).

European Parliament [EP] and Council (1997b), *Directive 97/33/EC of the European Parliament and of the Council on interconnection in telecommunications with regard to ensuring universal service and interoperability through application of the principles of open network pro*vision (ONP) (OJ L 199/32, 26.7.97).

Evans, Peter, Jacobson, Harold and Putnam, Robert (eds) (1993), *Double-Edged Diplomacy. International Bargaining and Domestic Politics* (Berkeley: University of California Press).

Foreman-Peck, James and Manning, Dorothy (1988), 'Telecommunications in Italy', in Foreman-Peck, James and Müller, Jurgen(ed), *European Telecommunications Organisation* (Baden-Baden: Nomos)

Foreman-Peck, James and Müller, Jurgen (eds) (1988), *European Telecommunications Organisation* (Baden-Baden: Nomos)

Gensollen, Michel (1991), 'Les réformes institutionnelles et réglementaires des télécommunications, *Communications & Stratégies*, 3: 17-34.

Grande, Edgar (1989), *Vom Monopol zum Wettbewerb?* (Wiesbaden: DUV).

Hattam, Victoria (1993), *Labor Visions and State Power. The Origins of Business Unionism in the United States* (Princeton: Princeton University Press).

Herguera, I and Stehmann, O (1997), 'Regulation and Competition Policy in the EU Telecommunications Industry', *Communications & Stratégies* no26, pp141-63

Héritier, Adrienne (1999), *After liberalization: public-interest services in the utilities* (Cambridge: Cambridge University Press)

Héritier, Adrianne, Knill, Christopher and Mingers, Susanne (1996), *Ringing the Changes in Europe. Regulatory Competition and Redefinition of the State. Britain, France, Germany* (Berlin and New York: Walter de Gruyter)

Hills, Jill (1986), *Deregulating Telecoms: competition and control in the United States, Japan and Britain* (London: Pinter).

Hooghe, Liesbet (ed) (1996), *Cohesion Policy and European Integration: Building Multi-Level Governance* (Oxford: Oxford University Press).

Hunt, Adrian (1997), 'Regulation of Telecommunications: the Developing EU Regulatory Framework and its Impact on the United Kingdom', *European Public Law*, 3(1): 93-115.

Ikenberry, John (1990), 'The International Spread of Privatisation Policies: Inducements, Learning and "Policy Bandwaggoning"' in EN Suleiman and J Waterbury (eds), *The Political Economy of Public Sector Reform and Privatization* (Oxford: Westview)

Immergut, Ellen (1992), *Health Politics: Interests and Institutions in Western Europe* (Cambridge: Cambridge University Press).

Jäger, Bernd (1994), 'Die Liestungsgüte des Telekommunikations-Übertragungswege-monopols in Deutschland auf dem Prüfstand', *Zeitschrift für Wirtschaftpolitik*, 43(3): 301-35.

Kay, John (1984), 'The Privatisation of BT', in Steel, D. and Heald, D. (eds), *Privatising Public Enterprises* (London: RIPA).

Koebberling, Uschi (1993), 'The Limits of National Governance. Regulatory Reform of Telecommunications in Canada and Germany'. *International Journal of Political Economy,* 23: 49-82.

Kolko, Gabriel (1977), *The Triumph of Conservatism: A Reinterpretation of American History 1900-1916* (New York: Free Press).

Larcher, Gérard (1993), *L'avenir du secteur des télécommunications*, rapport du Sénat no.129 (Paris: Sénat).

Larcher, Gérard (1996), *L'avenir de France Télécom: un défi national*, rapport du Sénat no.260 (Paris: Sénat).

Lawson, Nigel (1993), *The View from No.11* (London: Corgi).

Libois, Jean-Louis (1983), *Genèse et Croissance des Télécommunications* (Paris: Masson).

Longuet, Gérard (1988), *Télécoms. La Conquête de Nouveaux Espaces* (Paris: Dunod)

Majone, Giandomenico (1994), 'The Rise of the Regulatory State in Europe', *West European Politics*, 17(1): 77-101.

Majone, Giandomenico (1996), *Regulating Europe* (London: Routledge)

Marks, Gary (1993), 'Structural Policy and MultiLevel Governance in the European Community' in A Cafruny and G Rosenthal (eds), *The State of the European Community* (New York, Lynne Riener).

Marks, Gary (1997), 'An Actor-Centred Approach to Multi-Level Governance', *West European Politics,* 20(1).

Marks, Gary, Hooghe, Liesbet and Blank, K (1996), 'European Integration since the 1980s: State-Centric versus Multi-Level Governance', *Journal of Common Market Studies*, vol.34(4).

Maxwell, Winston (1996), 'Regulation and Competition: French Telecommunications Licensing', *Communications & Stratégies*, 22: 145-60.

McGowan, Francis and Wallace, Helen (1996), 'Towards a European regulatory state', *Journal of European Public Policy*, 3(4): 560-76.

Moon, Jeremy, Richardson, Jeremy, and Smart, Paul (1986), 'The privatisation of British Telecom: a case study of the extended process of legislation', *European Journal of Political Research*, 14: 339-55.

Mouline, A., 'Les stratégies internationales des opérateurs de télécommunications', *Communications & Stratégies*, 21 (1996), 77-93.

Natalicchi, Giorgio (1999), *The Take-Off of European Telecoms: Telecoms Policy and Integration Processes in the European Union* (Florence: manuscript)

Newman, Karen (1986), *The Selling of BT* (London: Holt Rinehart and Winston).

Noam, Eli (1989), 'International Telecommunications in Transition' in Crandall, R. W. and Flamm, K. (eds), *Changing the Rules: Technological Change, International Competition and regulation in Telecommunications* (Washington: Brookings)

Noam, Eli (1992), *Telecommunications in Europe* (New York: Oxford University Press)

Oftel (1994), *Annual Report 1994* (London: Oftel).

Oftel (1996a), *Annual Report 1996* (London: Oftel)

Oftel (1996b), *Oftel's proposals for Price Control and Fair Trading* (London: Oftel)

Prévot, Hubert (1989), *Rapport de synthèse* (Paris: PTE Ministry).

Putnam, Robert (1988), 'Diplomacy and domestic politics: the logic of two-level games', *International Organization,* 42(3): 427-60.

RegierungsKommission Fernmeldewesen (1987), *Neuordnung der Telekommunikation* (Heidelberg: von Decker).

Richardson, Jeremy (1996), *European Union. Power and Policy Making* (London: Routledge).

Richeri, Guiseppe (1985), 'The difficulties involved in the control and organization of telecommunications in Italy', *Media, Culture and Society*, 7: 49-70.

Robischon, Tobias (1999), *Telekommunikations-politik im deutschen Einigungsprozess* (Campus Verlag: Frankfurt and New York).

Rogy, Michel (1994), 'Price Cap Regulation in European Telecommunications', *Communications & Strategies,* 15: 47-75.

Roulet, Marcel [Président of France Télécom] (1994), *Rapport sur l'avenir du groupe France Télécom* (Paris: Ministère de l'Industrie, des Télécommunications et du Commerce Extérieur),

Sandholtz, Wayne (1992), *High-Tech Europe* (Berkeley, Los Angeles and Oxford: University of California Press).

Sandholtz, Wayne (1998), 'The Emergence of a Supranational Telecommunications Regime' in Sandholtz, Wayne and Stone Sweet, Alec (eds), *European Integration and Supranational Governance* (Oxford: Oxford University Press).

Sandholtz, Wayne and Stone Sweet, Alec (eds) (1998), *European Integration and Supranational Governance* (Oxford: Oxford University Press).

Sauter, Wolf (1995), 'The Telecommunications Law of the European Union', *European Law Journal*, 1(1): 92-111.

Sauter, Wolf (1997), *Competition Law and Industrial Policy in the EU* (Oxford: Clarendon Press).

Schmidt, Susanne (1991), 'Taking the long road to liberalization. Telecommunications reform in the Federal Republic of Germany', *Telecommunications Policy,* 15(3): 209-22.

Schmidt, Susanne (1996a), 'Commission activism: subsuming telecommunications and electricity under European competition law', *Journal of European Public Policy,* 16(3): 169-84.

Schmidt, Susanne (1996b), 'Privatizing the Federal Postal and Telecommunications Services' in Benz, Arthur and Goetz, Klaus H (eds), *A New Germany Public Sector? Reform, Adaptation and Stability* (Aldershot: Dartmouth).

Schmidt, Suzanne (1997), 'Sterile Debates and Dubious Generalisations: European Integration Theory Tested by Telecommunications and Electricity', *Journal of Public Policy,* 16(3): 233-71.

Schmidt, Vivien (1996), *From State to Market? The transformation of French business and government* (Cambridge: Cambridge University Press).

Schmidt, Vivien (2000), *Models of Industrial Capitalism* (forthcoming)

Schneider, Volker, Dang-Nguyen, Godefroy and Werle, Raymund (1994), 'Corporate Actor Networks in European Policy-Making: Harmonizing Telecommunications Policy', *Journal of Common Market Studies*, 32(4): 473-98.

Schneider, Volker and Werle, Raymund (1991), 'Policy Networks in the German Telecommunications Domain' in Marin, B and Mayntz, R (eds), *Policy Network-Empirical Evidence and Theoretical Considerations* (Frankfurt: Campus Verlag).

Scott, Colin and Audéoud, Olivier (eds) (1996), *EC Telecommunications Law* (Cologne: Bundesanzeiger-Verlag).

Stehmann, Oliver (1995), *Network Competition for European Telecommunications* (Oxford: Oxford University Press).

Steinmo, Sven (1993), *Taxation and Democracy* (New Haven and London: Yale University Press).

Stone Sweet, Alec and Sandholtz, Wayne (1998), 'Integration, Supranational Governance and the Institutionalization of the European Polity', in Sandholtz, Wayne and Stone Sweet, Alec (eds), *European Integration and Supranational Governance* (Oxford: Oxford University Press).

Thatcher, Mark (1992), 'Telecommunications in Britain and France: the Impact of National Institutions', *Communications et Stratégies*, 6: 35-62

Thatcher, Mark (1994), Organisational structure and regulatory reform: the extension of competition in Britain and France, *Journal of European Public Policy*, 1(3):128-50.

Thatcher, Mark (1995a), 'Regulatory Reform and Internationalization in Telecommunications', in Hayward, Jack E. S. (ed), *Industrial Enterprise and European Integration* (Oxford: Oxford University Press).

Thatcher, Mark (1995b), 'Institutional Reform and Transnational Forces for Change: the Case of Telecommunications in Britain and France', in *Jahrbuch für Europäische Verwaltungsgeschichte vol 7* (Baden-Baden: Nomos Verlagsgesellschaft).

Thatcher, Mark (1997), 'The Development of European Regulatory Frameworks: The Expansion of European Community Policy Making in Telecommunications' in

Stravridis, E, Mossialos, E, Morgan, R and Machin, H (eds), *New Challenges to the European Union.* (Aldershot: Dartmouth Publishing).

Thatcher, Mark (1999a), 'Liberalisation in Britain: From Monopoly to regulation of competition' in Eliassen, K. and Svojaag, M. (eds), *Liberalising European Telecommunications* (London, Routledge).

Thatcher, Mark (1999b), *The Politics of Telecommunications* (Oxford: Oxford University Press).

Thimm, AL (1992), *America's Stake in European Telecommunications Policies* (Westport: Quorum Books)

Ungerer, Herbert and Costello, Nicholas (1988), *Telecommunications in Europe* (Brussels: Commission of the European Communities).

Vogel, Stephen (1996), *Freer Markets, More Rules: Regulatory Reform in Advanced Industrial Countries* (Ithaca and London: Cornell University Press).

Wallace, Helen and Wallace, William (eds) (1996), *Policy Making in the European Union* (3rd ed; Oxford: Oxford University Press).

Weir, Margaret (1992), *Politics and Jobs. The Boundaries of Employment Policy in the United States* (Princeton: Princeton University Press).

Werle, Raymund (1990), *Telekommunikation in der Bundesrepublik* (Frankfurt and New York: Campus Verlag).

Werle, Raymund (1999), 'Liberalisation of Telecommunications in Germany' in Elliassen Kjell and Sjovaag, Marit (eds), *Liberalising European Telecommunications* (London, Routledge).

Wright, Vincent (ed) (1994), *Industrial Privatization in Western Europe* (London: Pinter)

CONFIGURATIONS OF ECONOMIC REGULATION IN THE EUROPEAN UNION: THE CASE OF ELECTRICITY IN COMPARATIVE PERSPECTIVE[1]

Burkard Eberlein
Technische Universität München
Lehrstuhl für Politische Wissenschaft

The powerful movement of privatization and liberalization in European Economies has not resulted in a simple retreat of the state (e.g. Müller/ Wright 1994). Governments are re-regulating privatized enterprises and liberalized markets (for telecommunications see Grande 1994, Thatcher this volume). The most prominent explanation for the paradox of "privatization and deregulation" was provided by Giandomenico Majone who identified a paradigm shift from the "positive" or interventionist state to the regulatory state, following the US-American example (Majone 1994a, 1994b, 1996, 1997; Seidman/ Gilmour 1986; Grande 1997). This shift has both a functional and a territorial dimension. Functionally, the post-Keynesian state adopts a different role in economic governance: from a role as producer of goods and services to that of a regulator of market processes. Territorially, the regulatory function is being promoted by the transfer of policy-making power to the EU, which largely operates as a regulatory state, and by EU influence on national policy-making.

The focus on broad trends like the 'rise of the regulatory state' should, however, not divert attention from specific variations of public regulation in the complex institutional environment of the EU multi-level system. This paper seeks to shed some light on the institutional complexity and variety of 'the' regulatory state in Europe (also see Eberlein 1998, 1999). The economic regulation of infrastructures and utilities serves as an example. I will focus more specifically on the case of across EU member states.

The paper is organized as follows. In a first part, I will briefly argue that dominant economic theories of regulation fail to capture the complex institutional nature and

---

[1] This contribution emerges from my collaboration in a comparative empirical research project ("Regulation and Infrastructures in Europe") directed by Professor Edgar Grande at the Technische Universität München. I wish to express my gratitude to Edgar for his generous support. A first version, which includes a detailed discussion of regulation theories and of Majone's thesis on the rise of the regulatory state in Europe, was presented to the panel "Regulation in Europe" at the ECSA Sixth Biennial International Conference, Pittsburgh, June 2-5, 1999. I wish to thank the participants for their helpful comments. Special thanks go to the discussant, Professor Giandomenico Majone. Copies of the initial draft are available on request with the author.

variation of the regulatory process. More sophisticated, political-institutionalist accounts are required which should use 'configurative analysis' based on comparative empirical research.

In a second, empirical part, I will illustrate the potential of such an approach by presenting the case of electricity regulation. I will map the dimensions of regulatory variation in the EU multi-level system (dependent variable). And I will try to identify configurative patterns of variables fit to explain the variation of regulatory regimes (independent variable).

(A) CONCEPTUALIZING (RE)-REGULATION

In retrospect, privatization and liberalization did not result in the simple retreat of the state, but rather in a redefinition of its role (Müller/ Wright 1994; Vogel 1996). Government re-regulation of privatized enterprises and liberalized markets in infrastructures basically flows from two different logics. First, regulation is supposed to correct market failures which arise or persist in the aftermath of privatization and liberalization. The 'non-contestable', physical network part of infrastructure systems is considered a 'natural monopoly', in which case the market fails to be the most efficient form of allocation (Berg/ Tschirhart 1988). Normative theories of regulation view market failures as justification for public intervention (Noll 1989). Either regulation seeks to substitute for or mimic the efficiency effects of competition or, if possible, it tries to create and protect competitive markets (economic logic of market-making). Second, regulation is used to promote social and political goals typically not served by competitive markets, by correcting the undesirable results of economic efficiency (political logic of market-correction). In practice, both logics cannot be clearly separated, but rather co-exist and may conflict (Prosser 1999: 199). More generally, as positive theories of regulation stress, regulation serves as a political arena for the distribution of costs and benefits, wherein competing interests and actors are mobilized.

Positive economic theories of regulation, which were developed on the basis of the long-standing US-American experience, focus on interest mobilization based on the distribution of costs and benefits, and on the bilateral relationship between the regulator and the regulated firm (Noll 1989; Baron 1995).[2] These theories are useful insofar as they

[2] The most familiar approach is **capture theory**, which holds that regulatory agencies are captured by the very economic interests they are supposed to regulate (Stigler 1971; Peltzman 1976). However, the prediction that a priori interests of regulators and the regulated firm will necessarily lead to capture by industry has not been confirmed in empirical testing (Wilson 1984; Derthick/ Quirk 1985). Capture theory was also questioned by studies conducted within the framework of **institutional economics**, which focuses on the **origin, choice and effectiveness of institutional arrangements**. The **principal-agent framework** directly addresses the problem of effective control raised by capture-theory (e.g. Weingast 1984; Shepsle/Weingast 1987). Regulation can be interpreted as a double principal-agent set-up. First, the regulatory agency needs to be held accountable to the political principal, through the use of effecient institutions which provide the agent with the appropriate incentives and sanctions so as not to 'shirk' its duty (e.g. Weingast/ Moran 1982). Second, the relationship between the regulatory agency and the regulated firm can be considered as a problem of control within a principal-agent framework. Again, the focus is on efficient institutions which, in this case, should be able to prevent agency capture by the

point to some general regulatory problems and challenges: effective control of both the regulated firm and the regulatory agency, and the design of efficient institutions to cope with the political pressures induced by the distributive effects of regulation.[3] However, formal economic models still tend to operate within a narrow framework of individualistic relationships between unitary actors. This perspective runs the danger of inviting flawed ex-post rationalizations of policy outcomes which are 'shown' to result from 'efficient' incentives and control patterns (see the critique by Eisner et al. 1996). Likewise, the public choice paradigm of utility maximization can be easily misused to rationalize, ex post, any regulatory outcome as the political equilibrium resulting from the interaction of utility-maximizing actors. Formal agency models do not pay sufficient attention to the complex institutional web which shapes the regulatory process. An exclusive focus, for example, on the bilateral regulatory contract between the regulator and the regulated firm misses both the internal organizational complexity of both parties and the external institutional and political context shaping their interaction.

Empirical studies of the U.S. regulatory process stress the variety of actors and factors impacting regulatory policy-making: agency staff, presidents, congressional committes, and courts (for example Moe 1985). More generally, regulatory politics does not escape the dynamics of the general political environment, such as changes in interest group politics (Eisner 1993; Reagan 1987). Political science writings on the politics of regulation have identified some important political-institutional factors shaping the regulatory process, for example the role of policy entrepreneurs (Wilson 1980) or the power of ideas (Derthick/ Quirk (1985)).

Compared to formal modelling, these kinds of accounts give a much more realistic picture. However, comprehensive reconstructions of the regulatory process run the opposite danger of "ending up with a sort of a-theoretical pluralism" (Prosser 1999: 205), with hardly any predictive and explanatory power. A viable alternative to formal modelling needs to be able to show which specific factors do explain a given regulatory outcome (and which factors do not), which of the stakeholders involved really matter and prevail, and why. In order to arrive at valid explanations, the different interests and strategies of politicians, regulators, and affected parties need to be systematically linked to relevant societal and institutional resources and constraints, as well as to the 'corridor' of available policy frames or repertoires (see the approach proposed by Snyder 1999: 178-179).

Neo-institutional writings provide some guidance to institutional factors with explanatory power in the analysis of economic governance across advanced industrial

---

regulated industry. A second approach within institutional economics is concerned with the reverse problem of governmental capture (or expropriation) by regulation. Its focus is on the protection of **property rights** of business investors, viewing regulation as a bilateral contract between the regulator and the regulated firm (e.g. Levy/ Spiller 1996; Troesken 1996). A detailed presentation and critique of these regulation theories can be found in Eberlein (1998: 7-10).

[3] There has been considerable progress in institutional economics towards more sophisticated models of the regulatory process, which try to incorporate complex institutional features and to deal with associated problems of incomplete information, the interaction dynamics of regulation, unforeseen contingencies, organizational complexity of regulation or multi-period or multi-principal set-ups of regulation (for an overview s. Baron 1995).

countries (e.g. Hall 1986; Scharpf 1991; Steinmo 1993; Wilks/ Wright 1987). These factors typically include: the structure and organization of decision-making and conflict resolution; the voting and party system; the organization of societal interests; and state traditions and normative policy concepts. The EU context introduces additional institutional variables to take into account, notably the multilevel character of decision-making and the high degree of interlacing of levels, institutions and policies (e.g. Marks et al. 1996).

Comparative empirical analysis provides the necessary grounding to political-institutionalist explanations. Obviously, this kind of enterprise is confronted with the familiar problem of "Too many variables, too few cases". In order to deal with this problem, my suggestion is to focus on a few, structured patterns or configurations of variables, rather than on a multitude of single variables. The basic idea of configurative analysis is that, while specific outcomes might only be explained by a specific (potentially unique) combination of variables, it is possible to relate observed variation in specific cases to some generally applicable rules or logics, so that there is no need to resort to ad-hoc accounts (Verba 1967; Lehmbruch et al. 1988). This kind of method seems particularly appropriate in a context characterized by complex interactions of variables and multiple causal pathways. Also, it allows for the detection of additional variables which were not recognized as important at the outset of a study.

Sophisticated comparative analysis recognizes that most social phenomena are not produced by a single cause but by specific combinations of causal variables. Furthermore, not only can specific constellations of variables produce different outcomes under different context conditions, but also different constellations may produce the same outcomes (Ragin 1987). In sum, careful configurative analysis of *variable interaction* is required.

In the second part of this paper, I will show how such a institutionalist-configurative perspective can inform the empirical analysis of economic regulation in the EU multi-level system. My modest intent is the following: first, to map out the different analytical dimensions of regulatory variation which deserve attention and require explanation. Second, to tentatively identify three configurative patterns of variables which seem fit to explain the variation found. I will use the electricity case in order to illustrate my argument, rather than to test causal propositions.

(B) ELECTRICITY REGULATION IN EUROPE: EU-FRAMEWORK AND VARIETY OF REGULATORY REGIMES

A closer look at the rise of 'the' regulatory state in Europe (Majone) reveals that public regulation as a new form of economic management comes in different shapes and sizes. The first dimension of variation, which is well established in the literature on economic governance (e.g. Campbell et al. 1991; Hollingsworth et al. 1994), is the sectoral one. In the field of infrastructure, two factors are of prime importance to explain inter-sectoral differences: the speed and scope of technological change and the degree of competition. Here, I will exclusively focus on the national dimension of variation within one sector.

1. LIBERALIZING EUROPEAN ELECTRICITY MARKETS

Electricity has some technical features typical for most utility systems: long-lived specific assets, dependence on integrated networks (the grid), and high co-ordination requirements. In addition, the two elements of fluctuating demand and non-storability combine to create the costly need to have sufficient capacity to equal or exceed load at all times. Given the non-substitutable nature of electricity, security of supply is of prime importance. Against this background, the entire sector has traditionally been considered a natural monopoly, requiring vertical system integration, the exclusion of competition and sustained state intervention.

The 1980s and 1990s have brought a world-wide, fundamental transformation of the power sector, with some Latin American (Chile, Argentina) and Anglo-American countries (New Zealand, Australia, Britain, U.S.A.) taking the lead (Gilbert/ Kahn 1996; Yajima 1997; OECD 1997; ICC 1998). The goal is to increase efficiency and drive down costs by introducing competition. Like in other network-based industries, the basic idea is to separate the "non-contestable" remnant of natural monopoly, i.e. the transmission and distribution wires as well as the grid management, from "contestable" generation and supply (Baumol et al. 1982). Apart from the neoliberal agenda of liberalization and deregulation, the movement to open up generation and supply to competition was also driven by some economic and technological developments.[4]

In Europe, the agenda of market-oriented reforms met with a heterogeneous landscape of national electricity management systems (McGowan 1996). The national power sectors differ with respect to a variety of factors: the mix of primary energy inputs into generation (coal, hydro, nuclear); the ratio of import dependence; ownership structure and the scope of monopoly rights; the extent to which the power sector was made to serve concerns of other sectors (environmental, industrial or employment policies) or larger political goals (national independence, military security, etc.). These differences resulted, for example, in substantiable variations in the costs of electricity. Speaking in ideal-types, one could distinguish, prior to market reforms, two different groups of electricity systems: the vertically integrated national monopolies (e.g. Britain and France), and the decentralised and fragmented systems (e.g. Germany), in which

---

[4] Already in the 1970s, changes in the costs of nuclear and coal-fired generation, the experience that independent power producers could operate without affecting the stability of an integrated grid, and the discovery that the minimum efficient scale of generation might be much smaller (questioning the assumption of economies of scale, and thus, of natural monopoly) combined to prepare market-oriented reforms. More recently, the development of the combined cycle gas turbine (CCGT) reduced the minimum efficient scale in generation and facilitated the decentralisation of generation, making smaller plants a viable option. Furthermore, advances in information technology reduced the costs of sophisticated metering and grid control equipment. This facilitated decentralization of supply, while making system co-ordination easier (OECD 1997: 162-164).

there is a complex mix of public and private ownership on different territorial levels (Cross 1996; Midttun 1997).

Against this background of national heterogeneity, the efforts of the European Commission to liberalize the network-based energy sector (electricity and gas), as part of the internal market program, encountered much more difficulties than in the case of telecommunications (Schmidt 1998; Eising/ Jabko 1999; Thatcher, in this volume). A long and winded policy process, set in motion with the 1988 Commission report on the "The internal market for energy", ended in a political compromise only in 1996. The Community directive 96/92/EC, adopted in December 1996, prescribes only an incremental and moderate opening of electricity markets to competition. In a first step, which took effect on February 19, 1999, the equivalent of the national share of large users (consumption exceeding 40 GWh/year), which corresponds to 26% of national electricity demand, was opened to competition. As from February 19, 2000, the threshold will go down to consumers using more than 20 GWh/year (28% of national demand), and further down to those using 9 GWh/year in 2003, which will open 33% of the market to competition. New generation capacity is open to competition without delay.

Many member states are moving faster than required by the EU directive (Klom 1997). Radical privatization of the British electricity industry started as early as 1989 and resulted in complete liberalization of markets. The Nordic countries also took the lead. Finland and Sweden started market opening in 1995 and 1996 respectively, following the 1991 Norwegian example. The big German market was completely liberalized in April 1998. The laggards are Belgium, Greece and Ireland, which gained exemption from the EU 1999 market opening for one or two more years. While it is estimated that almost two thirds of all European consumers are now able to choose their electricity supply freely, the overall picture is that of a differential process of liberalization.[5]

2. THE REGULATORY CHALLENGE

For competition to work in practice, the owners of the electricity networks, which remain natural monopolies, need to provide access to their lines to competitors. The transmission networks are usually owned by vertically integrated electricity companies, which also generate and sell electricity. Such companies will be tempted to discriminate in favour of their own group companies and against competitors. Therefore, effective competition crucially depends on non-discriminatory 'Third Party Access'. Viewed from the market failure perspective of economic efficiency (natural monopoly of transmission), this constitutes the main regulatory challenge after liberalization.

However, this is not the sole task of public regulation. As argued earlier, regulation has to deal with a variety of other social and political goals and interests. In the power sector, two concerns beyond economic efficiency play an important role. First, certain

[5] Much of the information used in this part was provided by the European Commission, DG XVII, Energy, Unit A3 (Functioning of the internal energy market), see also http://www.europa.eu.int/en/comm/dg17/dg17home.htm.

universal service standards continue to be applied: such as that all citizens are guaranteed electricity at fair prices, or that some vulnerable groups benefit from special conditions. Second, the protection of the environment remains a fundamental concern. Obviously, the political process brings in a variety of further interests: for example, the interest of employees in the ex-monopolists, which tend to reduce their workforce under the pressure of competition. Public service or environmental protection concerns need not, by necessity, conflict with the goal of economic efficiency in a liberalized market. But the distributive effects of sectoral restructuring and re-regulation are likely to create both winners and losers (who are not compensated out of efficiency gains generated by liberalization), and both have incentives to mobilize. Therefore, regulation is faced with the delicate task of balancing competing concerns and interests in a conflictual environment.

3. Variety and Resilience of National Patterns of Regulation

To analyse the variety of institutional solutions found for this regulatory challenge, it seems useful to distinguish between two dimensions of regulatory variation. The functional dimension is concerned with the scope and goals of regulation. The central question is how to balance competing concerns. The organizational dimension is about the design of regulatory institutions. The central question is who is to regulate, and on which territorial level regulation is to be carried out.

3.1. The Organizational Dimension

- National Room for Maneuver and Level Interaction

Electricity management in Europe is no longer a matter entirely left to the nation-states. Nor has the new regulatory function been simply moved to the EU level. Rather, a multi-tier fabric of public regulation is about to emerge. Roughly speaking, the distribution of competences looks like this: A framework, setting out minimum requirements and rules, is defined on the European level. The member states are given a large margin of choice as to how they seek to achieve the goals defined. For example, the electricity directive requires member states to ensure management unbundling of their transmission system operators and accounting separation of transmission (from distribution), so as to prevent discrimination against new competitors. But member states are free to chose between different forms of unbundling (creation of a separate legal entity or independence in management and accounting terms only). The same logic applies to the crucial question of third party access. The directive provides three alternative methods to achieve non-discriminatory access to electricity wires: regulated third party access, negotiated third party access and the so-called single buyer model.

According to the subsidiarity principle, a substantial portion of regulation is, thus, left to the member states, which are required by Article 22 of the EU directive to "create appropriate and efficient mechanismes for regulation, control and transparency". In principle, disputes in terms of network access are supposed to be settled by national regulatory bodies or competition authorities. This does not mean, though, that the European level does not play any active role besides setting out basic requirements. EU competition rules are applicable to the power sector. The competition directorate (DG IV) of the European Commission made it clear at the start of liberalization in early 1999 that it would increasingly devote itself to the electricity sector. But again, the pattern is not one of simple subordination of national policies. There is also a good deal of expertise-based exchange and cooperation between national and EU competition policies in the energy sector.

The Commission, while respecting the formal competencies granted to the member states, seeks to achieve uniform standards by facilitating the emergence of common regulatory philosophies: "While it is not appropriate to propose the harmonisation of regulatory approaches at the national level, an active policy through benchmarking is clearly appropriate. These objectives are pursued notably via the organisation of the bi-annual meeting of EU electricity regulatory forum in Florence" (European Commission 1999: 25). The Commission does not exclude the idea that for some issues vital for a common market in electricity, the soft instrument of encouraging common regulatory philosophies will not suffice. The current issue under review is cross-border transmission tarification, which can neither be simply delegated to the national level nor be sufficiently handled by ex-post EU competition law. To achieve an EU-wide tarification system, which is a prerequisite for the expected increase in cross-border trade to work properly, the Commission might proceed to propose "some new form of regulatory instrument" or the "establishment of a 'European Regulator'" (European Commission 1999: 27).

In sum, we find complex patterns of two-tier regulation (McGowan/ Wallace 1996), which go beyond a neat division of labor between the European and the national level (definition of framework versus implementation) and entail important interaction effects such as policy diffusion and regulatory learning.

- The Spectrum of National Resilience and Diversity

Nevertheless, the margin of choice left to Member States in the regulation of electricity markets remains substantial and results in different organizational solutions. To start with, the pre-regulation process of sectoral restructuring and liberalization looks quite different across countries. As far as the degree and timing of market opening is concerned, France is only about to implement the minimum requirements of the directive. This helps state monopolist EDF to secure a hardly contested home base from which to expand on markets which are fully liberalized like the German one.[6] Also, different avenues were chosen as regards the issues of restructuring and ownership structures.

---

[6] While the EU liberalization directive includes the principle of reciprocity (Art. 19(5)), this rule can be circumvented by the acquisition of company shares or subsidiaries in the foreign market targeted. This is the strategy of EDF in Germany where the company is currently bidding for a 25% share (to be sold by the *Land* Baden-Württemberg) of EnBW, one of the big German electric utilities.

Whereas some countries opted for restructuring the sector prior to liberalization, for example, by splitting up the national monopolist into different companies, in other countries liberalization happened on the basis of the given industry structure. These different starting points and choices have important effects, for example in terms of the division of efficiency gains between consumers and shareholders (in case of privatization).

National differences in regulatory set-up can be observed in various fields. In two-thirds of member countries, a separate legal entity was created to manage the network and grant access rights, while in the other countries, the transmission system operators are only independent in management and accounting terms from the generation and supply parts within a single electricity company. While most countries have opted for regulated third party access whereby tariffs for network use are fixed by relevant authorities and applied to all users, Germany (joined only by Greece and, temporarily, Danmark) chose negotiated third party access, wherein each user negotiates the terms of access with the system operator.

The national regulatory institutions put into place in the aftermath of liberalization exhibit important differences. National systems differ as to how they distribute regulatory powers between ministries, independent regulatory agencies or competition authorities. Most countries (except for Austria and Germany) established a sector-specific industry regulator with the power to regulate, ex ante, the prices and conditions charged by the transmission system operators. While in Austria, the Ministry of Economics holds ex-ante regulatory powers, only Germany relies on ex-post oversight by the national competition authority to prevent the abuse of monopoly power. Transmission rules and prices are not set by a regulatory authority, but are, in principle, the result of bilateral negotiations (negotiated third party access) between the system operator and the user. However, ground rules for access pricing and conditions were laid down in an industry agreement concluded between the VDEW (electricity companies), VIK (large industrial users), and the BDI (Federal Association of German Industry). This 'self-regulatory' agreement between peak associations works as a substitute for public regulation.

The strong role granted to industry associations in the German regime draws our attention to the fact that national patterns differ with respect to the power they give to the different stakeholders in the regulatory process. The organizational and procedural design of regulation affects the chances of different interests to participate in regulatory decision-making. This is an important link between the organizational and the functional dimension of regulation.

3.2. The Functional Dimension

The functional dimension of regulation, that is the scope and goals of regulation, is also subject to important variations. Both the EU framework and all national systems recognize that, while economic efficiency in the electricity sector is of greatest importance, this goal must co-exist not only with security of supply considerations but also with public service policy objectives, notably universal service and environmental protection.

- Market Efficiency and Public Service in the EU-Framework

The EU electricity directive enables member states to individually define public service obligations in the general economic interest, provided that they are objective, transparent and non-discriminatory, and that they fall into one of the following five categories: security of supply, regularity, quality and prices of supplies and environmental protection.

This is in line with the general recognition, laid down in the Amsterdam Treaty revisions, that 'services of general economic interest' play an important role "in promoting social and territorial cohesion" and that "the Community and the Member States (...) shall take care that such services operate on the basis of principles and conditions which enable them to fulfill their missions" (Art. 16). While this does not constrain the scope of the competition principle in any general way, it can be read as a "signal to the Commission, the Court and the legal profession that (...) more weight ought to be given to the purposes served by public service missions" (Scharpf 1997: 4). Earlier rulings of the Court of Justice (e.g. Alemelo and Corbeau cases) upholding the national imposition of a public service obligation on the basis of Art. 90, suggest that, in the legal space, too, the competition principle is being balanced by stressing alternative social values such as interregional equity in a national setting.

- Market Efficiency and Welfare Concerns on the National Level

The European framework thus accords member states considerable freedom to pursue, within certain limits, their own welfare concerns in electricity management. To be sure, market dynamics beyond the immediate control of regulatory authorities shape sectoral outcomes. The experience of pioneering countries (for the U.K. see Surrey 1996) as well as more recent developments in fully liberalized markets (Germany) suggest some common trends of development: price competition puts electricity companies under pressure to cut costs and reduce their workforce. Cost pressure favors co-operation between companies and concentration of market shares on an international level, with smaller or less efficient companies being driven from the market. Electricity becomes a commodity traded on a short-term, stock market basis, impacting the relative competitiveness of primary energy inputs.

However, the market logic remains subject to certain political decisions on the national level. Member states have developed different sets of specific provisions to achieve public service goals. In the realm of universal service and consumer protection, for instance, some countries go beyond the usual obligation to connect customers and to supply electricity on a regular basis, and require that 'captive' customers, who cannot buy at competitive prices, are charged 'reasonable prices' (Finland) or some 'maximum' price (Netherlands). Furthermore, some countries lay down special service provisions for the protection of the elderly and disabled customers (U.K.). In the field of environmental protection, different kinds of constraints are imposed on suppliers so as to ensure environmentally friendly forms of electricity production (e.g. Austria, Denmark).

Different methods are employed to support the use of renewable energy sources: direct investment subsidies and the obligation to purchase from small renewable producers (Sweden) or tax refunds and green pricing funds (Netherlands).

The new German energy law includes the potential possibility to refuse network access in order to protect production based on CHP[7] and renewables. Also, the energy laws continues the obligation for distributors to purchase electricity from renewable sources according to regulated feed in tariffs (*Stromeinspeisung*). Finally, Germany pursues a third welfare concern, namely to accommodate the special interests of the New *Länder*. It applied for a transitional regime to protect the investments for the construction and modernization of lignite power plants in East Germany. This regime would allow to refuse network access on the grounds that a sufficiently high level of power generation from lignite might be impaired.

More generally, countries have very different understandings of the nature of public service. In the French case, public service, as laid down in the electricity bill[8], is very broadly defined, including the requirement to contribute to "social cohesion" and to the "implementation of national policies, such as energy policy". Therefore, the type and scope of obligations imposed upon electricity undertakings look quite different from country to country.

Since in most countries, electricity re-regulation is a recent business, it remains to be seen how, over time, national regulatory bodies will balance competition with public service goals, and with which distributional effects for consumers, producers, and other affected interests. Regulatory practice will be influenced by the way public regulation is organized. This is because different types of regulatory bodies pursue different sets of goals, are more or less responsive to different kinds of interests, and are integrated in different ways into the EU multi-level fabric. To give an example: it seems reasonable to assume that competition authorities will give more weight to the single goal of competition, while sector-specific ministries will be more inclined or pressured to take a variety of social and political goals into consideration.

4. Explaining Variation: The Trias of Configurative Patterns

How to explain the variety of regulatory regimes? I propose to focus on three configurations of institutional variables. The first one is structure-oriented, looking at the organization of political authority and decision-making. The second one is process-oriented, focusing on state-society relations and interest representation. The third is about the 'belief systems' and 'policy frames' which inform the substance of regulatory choice.

[7] Combined Heat and Power (*Kraft-Wärme-Kopplung*)

[8] The bill was adopted on 2 March 1999 by the National Assembly (http://www.senat.fr/leg/taan98-253.html).

4.1. Structures of Political Organization

Regulatory policy-making is embedded in larger structures of political organization which influence the design of regulatory institutions and the nature of the regulatory process. A good case in point is how the features of the EU multi-level system shape the organizational architecture of European electricity regulation.

As a rule, EU liberalization is driven by the supranational dynamic of 'negative integration' (market opening), which enjoys both a strong legal and ideological footing, rather independent of member state control.[9] 'Positive integration', that is re-regulation on the EU level, by contrast, is very difficult to achieve because its depends on a political consensus among member states. It is true that the EU has been quite successful in establishing policies and agencies concerned with social regulation (environment, health, safety of the workplace). This success is possible because social regulation is about product- or mobility-related rules which complement the market-creating logic of negative integration. Economic regulation is a different matter. It makes rules concerning the conditions of production, bringing the starkly different economic conditions in Europe, and, thus, diverging member states interests into play and conflict. This is a major obstacle to regulation on the European level.

This institutional context helps to explain why there is no simple centralization of regulatory functions at the EU level and shifts attention to the patterns of level interaction instead. The fact that EU-level actors, like the Commission, seek to influence national regulatory policy-making by creating informal networks disseminating knowledge and 'good practice' (take the Electricity Regulation Forum mentioned above as an example) can be attributed to the fact that the EU lacks hierarchical regulatory powers. Regulation by networks (Dehousse 1997), policy diffusion and regulatory learning play an important role. But multi-level interaction might also encourage more negative effects such as administrative competition or deadlock. It is a matter of empirical inquiry to identify relevant patterns of level linkages in different policy areas. For a better theoretical grounding and understanding of EU multi-level governance it is of prime importance to understand the underlying interorganizational logic of arena and level linkages, of arena coupling and de-coupling (for the case of regional policies see Benz/ Eberlein 1999).

On the national level, too, the structures of political organization will shape regulatory design and process. One important dimension is the degree of (vertical) centralization and (horizontal) concentration of decision-making powers. In federal Germany, for example, local governments as well as *Länder* authorities traditionally play an important ownership and management role in the national electricity system which is characterized by territorial fragmentation (Schiffer 1999). Next to the big eight

---

[9] In the sensitive case of electricity, however, member state opposition to liberalization was very strong, so that the Commission did not use its legal powers, and a compromise in the European Council had to be found. Eising/Jabko (1999) argue that liberalization was not the simple result of intergovernmental bargaining but that it happened because key domestic actors in France and Germany changed their preferences in favour of liberalization. For the distinction between negative and positive integration, see Scharpf 1996.

interconnected utilities, which control most of the generation in their area, there are about 80 regional and some 800 local utilities (400 of which involved in generation).

The new regulatory regime does not break with this regional tradition by creating a central regulatory agency on the federal level, but continues to grant some regulatory powers to *Länder* authorities, next to fully exposing the sector to national competition law monitored by the federal competition authority. The Federal Ministry of Economics remains in charge of general policy formulation. Municipal actors who, thanks to party-political and territorial channels, have a powerful voice in the national arena, had opposed market liberalization. They feared municipal utilities (*Stadtwerke*) would lose out in the competition with the big utilities. The temporary authorization of the single-buyer model as an alternative model of grid access, next to Negotiated Third Party Access, granted until 2005 by the new legislation, was designed to somewhat protect municipal interests. This did, however, not stop liberalization.

Actually, fierce price competition, which, very recently, has begun to seize the market for smaller consumers (households), too[10], is about to erode monopoly profits which municipal authorities had used to cross-subsidize other local services (transport), to maintain jobs and to promote environmentally friendly ways of generation.[11] Currently, public sector unions and Social-Democratic MPs lobby the Federal Minister of Economics to revise the energy law and exempt municipal utilities from unfettered competition, so as to protect decentral supply structures.[12] Given the strong market dynamic and freshly stirred consumer awareness, it seems unlikely, however, that liberalization will simply be reduced to the minimum level required by the EU directive. This is also because alternative, 'competition-friendly' instruments to cater for certain public service concerns (e.g. environmentally-friendly production), voiced by local utilities, are available, such as regulated feed-in tariffs or obligations to purchase from renewable and CHP producers or green tax schemes.

A strong horizontal concentration of decision-making powers with few 'veto players' able to obstruct the will of the political executive, and few legal constraints on the exercise of these powers, gives the government of the day substantial powers to intervene into or rearrange the regulatory regime. In the British case, for example, the incoming Labour Government, which had picked upon public indignation over 'excessive utility profits' when in opposition, imposed a one-time 'windfall tax' aimed to recoup the 'super profits' which the utilities and their shareholders had reaped, immediately following

---

[10] After substantial price cuts (about 30%) for industrial customers in 1998/1999, the summer of 1999 saw a first round of price competition for household consumers between new competitors and the established big utilities. Large-scale, aggressive marketing campaigns signalled to every consumer: electricity is a commodity, and you now have the choice between different offers and suppliers (see The Economist, August 28th 1999, p. 51-52; Handelsblatt, August 12th 1999, p. 18).

[11] However, only a minority of municipal utilities (*Stadtwerke*) actually generate a substantial part of the electricity they sell. (And even less do so on the basis of environmentally-friendly CHP). Only this group clearly suffers from competition whereas as those which buy from the big utilities actually can benefit from it. Moreover, as mentioned earlier, current legislation already provides the possibility for *Stadtwerke* to refuse network access in order to protect investments in CHP production. It is true, however, that the big utilities see liberalization as the welcome opportunity to make inroads into local supply areas. It is expected that the current territorial patchwork of 800 *Stadtwerke* will be considerably reduced.

[12] See Süddeutsche Zeitung, September 14th 1999, p. 23.

privatization. To be sure, the transition to a new, post-privatization regulatory regime has rather led to a certain fragmentation of executive powers, with the rise of independent regulatory agencies who share powers with the Secretary of State and the national competition authorities (Thatcher 1998). However, British traditions of executive concentration of powers prevail insofar as individual industry regulators have been vested with enormous powers, while regulatory discretion is subject to few procedural or material constraints. Consequently, individual regulators have established themselves at the center of the regulatory process. A telling example from electricity regulation is the dramatic March 1995 volte-face revision of electricity prices, which had only previously been fixed in August 1994. The regulator Littlechild decided to tighten the price cap after the defense of one of the 12 Regional Electricity Companies, Northern Electric, to a takeover bid revealed "that the company was far wealthier than the regulator and the public had appreciated" (Sturm/ Wilks 1997: 31).

4.2. State-Society Relations

The second, more process-oriented pattern of variables looks at the organization of societal interests and established patterns of interaction between public and private actors, in which the relationship between public regulator and private regulatee are embedded. In particular, it refers to different forms of interest representation and mediation.

The organization of societal interests plays a double role in shaping the regulatory process. First, the process of sectoral restructuring and liberalization reflects the relative power of different interests. For example, in some countries, vertically integrated electricity undertakings were strong enough to prevent pro-competitive disintegration (structural unbundling) and the transfer of electricity wires to an independent grid company. Obviously, such a transfer is more difficult to achieve under conditions of fragmented, private grid ownership, but countries with former national monopolists also differ in this respect (e.g. Britain and Sweden versus France).

Another case in point is the variable distribution of costs and benefits by sectoral restructuring and liberalization. In the British case, the initial 'regulatory contract' struck between the government and the electricity companies strongly favoured the interests of companies' executives and utility shareholders and investors (Veljanovski 1991). This contract reflected the converging interest of the incumbents' management and the government to make privatization a success at the stock market. By way of contrast, the electricity bill in the French case protects the privileged position of the former monopolist's workforce, by requiring that future competitors must grant equivalent social and labor rights to their employees. This provision reflects the relative strength of trade unions in the restructuring process.

Second, societal interests considerably influence the exercise of regulatory powers. A good example is the German regulatory regime. As outlined earlier, established industry associations successfully pressed for 'self-regulatory' powers to define the rules for grid access in an agreement which works a substitute for public regulation of third-party access. To be sure, the Conservative government of the day also declined to erect detailed rules for network access in order to bypass the *Bundesrat*, the Second Chamber, which was dominated by the opposition parties.[13] However, it is important to understand that associational self-regulation is in tune with established traditions of sectoral governance. Unlike in the German telecommunications sector, which, prior to liberalization, was dominated by a national monopolist and ministry, rule-making in electricity did not revolve around the competent bureaucracy (the Federal Ministry of Economics). Rather, it emerged from intermeshed private-public networks between electricity businesses and associations on the one hand and state and municipal actors on the other hand, who all benefited from monopoly profits. These different sectoral traditions or paths were not simply abandoned after EU-driven liberalization. In telecoms, an independent regulatory agency, that is: a de-facto organizational successor to the former national Ministry, was established. In electricity, by contrast, a much stronger self-regulatory role was granted to key associations of the old sectoral regime.

The above mentioned industry agreement (*Verbändevereinbarung*) to manage network access, struck in May 1998, was criticized (not least by the European Commission) for including distance-related elements in the pricing principles for transmission fees and for tailoring transmission rules exclusively to the needs of large industrial users, in short: for giving pride of place to established sectoral actors. The needs of smaller consumers (households) and of new market actors (e.g. energy brokers, 'green' traders) as well as new market requirements (pool, spot and stock market trading) were not sufficiently taken into account. The temporary agreement, due to elapse by October 1st, 1999, is being renegotiated at the moment, amid calls, from different corners, for the establishment of an independent regulator. The Ministry of Economics has stressed repeatedly, however, that it trusts industry associations to come to a satisfactory revision of the agreement, and that the creation of an industry regulator would only be an option in case of complete failure to renew the *Verbändevereinbarung*. It is supported in this view by the Federal Cartel Office which would not like to share oversight powers with a new (and potentially less competition-friendly) industry regulator.

This example illustrates how established patterns of interest representation mould regulatory processes. Different types of state-society relations can be expected to have different impacts upon the nature and outcome of the regulatory process (Wilks/ Wright 1987). In pluralist systems, for instance, one would expect the relationship between regulatory agencies and regulated industries to be rather formalized and distant, or even conflictual. The risk of capture seems rather low, but compliance costs might be high due to the conflictual nature of the regulatory process. In corporatist systems, which build on close relationships of exchange and cooperation between state agencies and a small number of businesses, regulation should be much less conflictual, but will systematically exclude interests (e.g. competitors and small consumers) which are not part of the corporatist network.

[13] These access rules would have required the consent of the *Bundesrat*, and could thus have stalled the reform process.

4.3. The Power of Ideas

Third, and finally, regulatory policy-making is not only influenced by institutional and societal resources and constraints, but also by certain sets of ideas and 'policy frames'. Ideas have been recognized as key independent variables in the policy process shaping agenda-setting and the choice of policy options (e.g. Hall 1993). Regulatory philosophies and frames are particularly important when it comes to substantive issues of regulation. As we have seen, the EU framework of electricity regulation leaves policy-makers considerable margins to opt for different packages of goal balancing. The relative weight policy-makers accord to competing concerns is influenced by deeply entrenched state traditions (Dyson 1980) and 'belief systems' (Sabatier 1988) defining the proper role of the state and the scope of public responsibilities.

The classical example mentioned above is the concept of public service, which is interpreted in very different ways across countries. In the French Republican tradition, for example, 'service public' is an essential principle and a mission to be guaranteed by the state (Bauby 1997). The French electricity bill defines the entire sector as "service public de l'électricité". The stated aim of new legislation is to combine the strengthening of the public service of electricity with the introduction of "some controlled elements of competition".

In the Anglo-Saxon context, by contrast, the competition principle ranks much higher. While competition is the overriding principle, the course of action pursued by individual industry regulators is also shaped by specific economic-philosophical backgrounds and schools of thought. One of the architects of British utility regulation, Professor Littlechild, who later was appointed electricity regulator, can be shown to be guided by the Austrian school of economic thinking, though, in practice, his approach had unintended consequences (Burton 1997).

Finally, the German discourse of "social market economy" calls for a rather broad inclusion of welfare concerns in infrastructure management, a factor which might at least cushion the social effects of the current commodification of infrastructure services. The normative frame of organized market capitalism legitimates a strong input of established sectoral interests in regulatory decision-making.

To be sure, policy paradigms or frames are often used to advance specific interests. Also, they are not inert but might evolve over time. The definition of policy frames is an important way to exercise 'soft' power and shape the direction and outcomes of policies. The efforts of the European Commission to establish common standards of 'good regulatory practice' in electricity regulation is a good example. The opening of a new policy arena (re-regulation after liberalization) creates a policy window for actors to set the agenda, by providing frames of 'good policy'.

It is by careful empirical analysis of case-specific interactions of structural, process and idea-based, general patterns that we can arrive at explanations of why and how specific regulatory regimes emerge and may resist pressures for convergence. The current German system of electricity regulation, for example, which relies on associational self-regulation of grid access, can be shown to result from the interaction of a decentralized and fragmented political system with a system of state-society relations, in which societal actors are granted a 'private government' role in sectoral management, underscored by the normative frame of organized market capitalism.

(C) CONCLUSIONS

Economic Regulation in Europe in the aftermath of EU–driven liberalization is characterized by considerable institutional complexity and variation. Despite some market and EU pressures for convergence, a variety of national (and sectoral) regulatory regimes persist. I tried to map the dimensions of regulatory variation, using the example of electricity regulation across EU member states. Dominant economic theories of regulation fail to capture the variety of the regulatory process in the EU multi-level context. Therefore, I introduced 'configurative analysis', based on comparative empirical research, as a more promising avenue of inquiry. Finally, I identified and illustrated three patterns of institutional variables designed to explain the variety of regulatory regimes.

However, the job to test specific causal propositions remains to be done. Also, once the variation of regulatory regimes or solutions has been explained, future comparative research faces still another challenge: To analyse if and how different regulatory regimes really make a difference in terms of policy outcomes.

REFERENCES

Baron, David: The economics and politics of regulation: perspectives, agenda, and approaches. In: Jeffrey S. Banks and Eric A. Hanushek (eds.), *Modern Political Economy*, Cambridge, 10-62.

Bauby, Pierre, 1997: *Le service public*, Paris.

Baumol, William J., John C. Panzar and Robert Willig, 1982: *Contestable Markets and the Theory of Industry Structure*, New York.

Benz, Arthur and Burkard Eberlein, 1999: The Europeanization of regional policies: patterns of multi-level governance. In: *Journal of European Public Policy* 6, 329-348.

Berg, Sanford V. and John Tschirart, 1988: *Natural Monopoly Regulation: Principles and Practice*, Cambridge.

Burton, John, 1997: The Competitive Order or Ordered Competition? The 'U.K. Model' of Utility Regulation in Theory and Practice. In: *Public Administration* 75, 7-58.

Campbell John L., Joseph R. Hollingsworth and Leon N. Lindberg (eds), 1991: *Governance of the American Economy*, Cambridge.

Cross, Eugene D., 1996: *Electric Utility Regulation in the European Union. A Country by Country Guide*, Chichester.

Dehousse, Renaud, 1997: Regulation by networks in the European Community: the role of European agencies. In: *Journal of European Public Policy* 4, 246-261.

Derthick, Martha and Paul J. Quirk, 1985: *The Politics of Deregulation*, Washington.

Dyson, Kenneth 1980: *The State Tradition in Western Europe*, Oxford.

Eberlein, Burkard, 1998: *Regulating Public Utilities in Europe: Mapping the Problem.* Florence (EUI Working Paper RSC No. 98/31).

Eberlein, Burkard, 1999: L'Etat régulateur en Europe. In: *Revue Française de Science Politique*, 49, 205-230.

Eising, Rainer and Nicolas Jabko, 1999: *Moving Targets: Institutional Embeddedness and Domestic Politics in the Liberalization of EU Electricity Markets* (Paper prepared for the Sixth Biennial International Conference of the European Community Studies Association, Pittsburgh, June 2-5, 1999).

Eisner, Marc A., 1993: *Regulatory Politics in Transition*, Baltimore.

Eisner, Marc A., Jeff Worsham and Evan Ringquist, 1996: Crossing the Organizational Void: The Limits of Agency Theory in the Analysis of Regulatory Control. In: *Governance* 9, 407-428.

European Commission, 1999: *Second Report to the Council and the European Parliament on Harmonisation Requirements* (Directive 96/92/EC concerning common rules for the internal market in electricity), COM (1999) 164 final, Brussels (16.04. 1999).

Gilbert, Richard J. and Edward P. Kahn (eds), 1996: *International Comparisons of Electricity Regulation*, Cambridge.

Grande, Edgar, 1994: The New Role of the State in Telecommunications. An International Comparison. In: *West European Politics* 17, 138-157.

Grande, Edgar, 1997: Vom produzierenden zum regulierenden Staat: Möglichkeiten und Grenzen von Regulierung bei Privatisierung. In: Klaus König/ Angelika Benz (eds.), *Privatisierung und staatliche Regulierung. Bahn, Post und Telekommunikation, Rundfunk*, Baden-Baden, 576-591.

Hall, Peter, 1986: *Governing the Economy: The Politics of State Intervention in Britain and France*, Cambridge.

Hall, Peter, 1993: Policy Paradigms, Social learning and the State: the Case of Economic Policy-making in Britain. In: *Comparative Politics* 25, 275-294.

Hollingsworth, J. Rogers, Philippe C. Schmitter and Wolfgang Streeck (eds), 1994: *Governing Capitalist Economies. Performance and Control of Economic Sectors*, New York.

ICC (International Chamber of Commerce), 1998: *Liberalization and Privatization of the Energy Sector.* Full Report, Paris.

Klom, Andy M., 1997: Effects of Deregulation Policies on Electricity Competition in the EU. In: *Journal of Energy and Natural Resources Law* 15, 1-22.

Lehmbruch, Gerhard, Otto Singer, Edgar Grande and Marian Döhler, 1988: Institutionelle Bedingungen ordnungspolitischen Strategiewechsels im internationalen Vergleich. In: Manfred G. Schmidt (ed.), *Staatstätigkeit* (PVS-Sonderheft 19), Opladen, 251-283.

Levy, Brian and Pablo T. Spiller, 1996: A Framework for Resolving the Regulatory Problem. In: Brian Levy and Pablo T. Spiller (eds.), *Regulations, Institutions, and Commitment. Comparative Studies of Telecommunications*, Cambridge, 1-35.

Majone, Giandomenico, 1994a: Paradoxes of Privatization and Deregulation. In: *Journal of Public Policy* 13, 53-69.

Majone, Giandomenico, 1994b: The Rise of the Regulatory State in Europe. In: Wolfgang C. Müller and Vincent Wright (eds.): *The State in Western Europe. Retreat or Redefinition?*. Ilford, 77-101.

Majone, Giandomenico, 1996: *Regulating Europe*, London.

Majone, Giandomenico, 1997: From the Positive to the Regulatory State: Causes and Consequences of Changes in the Mode of Governance. In: *Journal of Public Policy* 17, 139-67.

Marks, Gary, Fritz W. Scharpf, Philippe C. Schmitter and Wolfgang Streeck (eds.), 1996: *Governance in the European Union*, London.

McGowan, Francis (ed.), 1996: *European Energy Policies in a Changing Environment*, Heidelberg.

McGowan, Francis and Helen Wallace, 1996: Towards a European Regulatory State. In: *Journal of European Public Policy* 3, 560-576.

Midttun, Atle (ed.), 1997: *European Electricity Systems in Transition. A Comparative Analysis of Policy and Regulation in Western Europe*, Oxford.

Moe, Terry, 1985: Control and Feedback in Economic Regulation: The Case of the NLRB. In: *American Political Science Review* 79, 1094-1116.

Müller, Wolfgang C. and Vincent Wright (eds.), 1994: *The State in Western Europe. Retreat or Redefinition?* Ilford.

Noll, Roger G., 1989: Economic Perspectives on the Politics of Regulation. In: Richard Schmalensee and Robert D. Willig (eds.), *Handbook of Industrial Organization*, Vol. II, Amsterdam, 1254-1287.

OECD, 1997: The OECD Report on Regulatory Reform, *Vol. I: Sectoral Studies*, Paris.

Peltzman, Sam, 1976: Toward a More General Theory of Regulation. In: *Journal of Law and Economics* 19, 211-240.

Prosser, Tony, 1999: Theorising Utility Regulation. In: *Modern Law Review* 62, 196-217.

Ragin, Charles C., 1987: *The Comparative Method. Moving Beyond Qualitative and Quantitative Strategies*, Berkeley.

Reagan, Michael D., 1987: *Regulation. The Politics of Policy*, Boston.

Sabatier, Paul A., 1988: An Advocacy Coalition Framework of Policy Change and the Role of Policy-oriented Learning therein. In: *Policy Science* 21, 129-168.

Scharpf, Fritz W., 1991: *Crisis and Choice in European Social Democracy*, Ithaca.

Scharpf, F.W., 1996: Negative and Positive Integration in the Political Economy of European Welfare States, in: Gary Marks, Fritz W. Scharpf, Philippe C. Schmitter and Wolfgang Streeck (eds.), *Governance in the European Union*, London, 15-39.

Scharpf, Fritz W., 1997: *Balancing Positive and Negative Integration: The Regulatory Options for Europe*. MPIfG Working Paper 97/8, November 1997, Cologne.

Schiffer, Hans-Wilhelm, 1999: *Energiemarkt Bundesrepublik Deutschland*, Cologne.

Schmidt, Susanne K., 1998: Commission Activism: Subsuming telecomunications and electricity under European competition law. In: *Journal of European Public Policy* 5, 169-184.

Seidman, Harold/ Robert Gilmour, 1986: *Politics, Position and Power. From the Positive to the Regulatory State*, 4th edition, Oxford.

Shepsle, Kenneth A. and Barry R. Weingast, 1987: The Institutional Foundations of Committee Power. In: *American Political Science Review* 81, 85-104.

Snyder, Richard, 1999: After Neoliberalism. The Politics of Reregulation in Mexico. In: *World Politics* 51, 173-204.

Steinmo, Sven, 1993: *Taxation and Democracy. Swedish, British and American Approaches to Financing the Modern State*, New Haven.

Stigler, George J., 1971: The Theory of Economic Regulation. In: *Bell Journal of Economics and Management Science* 2, 1-21.

Sturm, Roland and Stephen Wilks, 1997: *Competition Policy and the Regulation of the Electricity Supply Industry in Britain and Germany (Anglo-German Foundation for the Study of Industrial Society)*, London.

Surrey, John (ed.), 1996: *The British Electricity Experiment. Privatization: the Record, the Issues, the Lessons*, London.

Thatcher, Mark, 1998: Institutions, Regulation, and Change: New Regulatory Agencies in the British Privatised Utilities. In: *West European Politics* 21, 120-147.

Troesken, Werner, 1996: *Why Regulate Utilities?*, Ann Arbor.

Veljanovski, Cento, 1991: The Regulation Game. In: ders. (ed.), *Regulators and the Market. An Assessment of the Growth of Regulation in the U.K.*, London, 3-28.

Verba, Sydney, 1967: Some Dilemmas of Comparative Research. In: *World Politics* 20, 111-127.

Vogel, Steven K., 1996: *Freer Markets, More Rules. Regulatory Reform in Advanced Industrial Countries*, Ithaca.

Weingast, Barry R., 1984: The Congressional-Bureaucratic System: A Principal Agent Perspective. In: *Public Choice* 44, 147-191.

Weingast, Barry R. and Mark J. Moran, 1982: The Myth of the Runaway Bureaucracy: The Case of the FTC. In: *Regulation* 6, 22-28.

Wilks, Stephen and Maurice Wright (eds.), 1987: *Comparative Government-Industry Relations. Western Europe, the United States, and Japan*, Oxford.

Wilson, James Q., 1980: The Politics of Regulation. In: James Q. Wilson (ed.), *The Politics of Regulation*, New York, 357-394.

Wilson, Graham K., 1984: Social Regulation and Explanations of Regulatory Failure. In: *Political Studies* 32, 203-225.

Yajima, Masayuki, 1997: *Deregulatory Reforms of the Electricity Supply Industry*, Westport, CT.

THE RISE OF THE COMPETITION STATE: THE DYNAMICS OF BRITISH AND AMERICAN TELECOM AND ELECTRICITY REGIMES

David Levi-Faur
University of Haifa and
Center for European Politics, Economics and Society, Oxford University

"Regulation and competition are rhetorical friends and deadly enemies: over the doorway of every regulatory agency... should be carved: Competition Not Admitted"
(George Stigler, 1971)

Change, global or local, is an omnipresent phenomenon nowadays: it leaves its mark everywhere and challenges us to study it both empirically and theoretically. One of the most challenging lines of inquiry, in the study of change, is Giandomenico Majone's notion of the transformation of the positive (interventionist) state into a regulatory state. In Majone's conceptualization, the past is represented by the "Positive State" but the future belongs to the "Regulatory State" - with its new structure of governance and its new political strategies (Majone, 1997). While the nature and timing of change have varied a good deal from country to country, the changes are compelling and far-reaching (Majone, 1997, 143). The transformation from a positive state to a regulatory state is expressed in a shift: from taxing and spending to rule making; from centralized bureaucracy to autonomous agencies; from party and parliamentary politics to legalistic and professional politics; from corporatist to pluralist political culture; and from direct to indirect political accountability. Majone's conceptualization is especially intriguing because it integrates insights and knowledge from public administration, public policy, and theories of political economy (See also, Majone, 1990; 1991; 1994; 1996).

Majone characterizes the positive and regulatory states by their major policy tools. The positive state is characterized by policies of intervention, taxing, and spending, and by emphases on "redistributive policies and discretionary management of aggregate demand". According to Majone, these policies represent the "social democratic consensus about the beneficent role of the positive state - as planner, direct producer of goods and services, and employer of last resort" (Majone, 1997, 141). The positive state is, according to Majone, a post-war phenomenon, and he sometimes also calls it also an interventionist state. The importance of redistributive policies and discretionary management of demand is revealed by the similar label of the Keynsian Welfare State. The economic crisis of the 1970s was the turning point in the shift towards a new form of political-economic order, characterized by the privatization of public corporations on the one hand and the rise of regulatory structures and tools on the other. Regulation, it seems, is not perceived as a positive policy tool; it is adopted not on its own merits but as a protective and defensive tool. It is a substitute for macroeconomics, stabilization policies, and redistribution policies (the three main types of public intervention in the economy) that are less viable in today's Europe. The regulatory state is identified with rule making and the correction of "various types of 'market failure': monopoly power, negative externalities, incomplete information, insufficient provision of public goods" (Majone, 1997, 141). The rise of regulation as a mode of governance is promoted by regulatory competition between states with the effect of "limiting the role of the interventionist or positive state" (Majone, 1997, 140).

There are direct positive relations between strategy and structure in Majone's conceptualization of the changes. Concentration of several basic strategies such as privatization, liberalization, and deregulation (regulatory reform) result in the creation of a new political structure, namely the regulatory state. This formulation of the relation between political strategies and political structures follows Alfred Chandler, who argued that "structure follows strategy and... the most complex type of structure is the result of the concatenation of several basic strategies" (Chandler, 1962, 14). In other words, the result of the liberal strategies is the creation of regulatory structures, which are liberal rather than social-democrat and which are aimed to the correction of market failures rather than at the administration of direct provision of services. Majone's thesis of the transformation from positive to regulatory is applied to Europe but is inspired by American terminology and particular trajectory of state formation. Specifically, his analysis draws on the fourth edition of *Politics, Position and Power: From the Positive to the Regulatory State*, which deals with the administrative reforms in the US (Seidman and Gilmour, 1986).

While Majone provides an important insight into the dynamics of change - especially the emphasis on the growth of regulatory policies and the existence of "regulatory competition" between nations - his analysis should be refined in regard to four important issues. Firstly, Majone's conceptualization of change is more acceptable when he deals with *strategies* (deregulation, privatization, liberalization, etc.) and less so when he deals with *structures* (the institutional setting in which these strategies occur). This paper aims to present an alternative conceptualization of the relations between strategy and structure, which draws on historical institutionalism (Steinmo, Thelen and Longstreth, 1992). Secondly, while Majone grounds his analysis in the American regulatory experience, his terminology - particularly the notion of rise of the regulatory state on the national level - excludes the American trajectory of change, and especially some important commonalties and processes of policy emulation across the world. The United States, after all, has been *the* Regulatory State since the late 19th century. Thus, comprehensive conceptualization of change - one which can deal with the divergent state trajectories in US and Europe -

cannot take the past simply as a positive state and cannot conceptualize current changes in the United States simply as the rise of a regulatory state. This paper's suggestion is to characterize the British experience (and in this regard also the European developments) as a change from a Service-provision state to a Competition state. The American experience of change in the last century is best characterized as a change from a Regulatory State to a Competition state.

Thirdly, this paper suggests that there are intimate and positive-sum relations between regulation and competition as well as between the rise of regulatory state and the rise of the Competition State. The competition state, critically relying on regulation-for-competition, may be as interventionist as past state structures. This point is not clearly emphasized by Majone and is in clear disagreement with the rhetoric of deregulation that characterizes the Anglo-American discourse of change and is reflected in the citation of George Stigler cited at the beginning of this paper.

Fourthly, unlike Majone this paper characterizes the regulatory state as a positive (interventionist welfare-oriented) state. It is argued that the rise of ordered competition (that is, competition critically sustained by regulation) may result in the same or even better social welfare than in the case of etatist regimes (interventionist, state monopoly over public goods). Social achievements of etatist regimes are only partly challenged, the outcomes of these challenges are not necessarily pre-determined, and most important, the new regimes open new social options. This is one essential reason why the conceptualization of today's "global change" should be of a "change within the state" and not a "change of the state". The regulatory institutions that govern the current regulatory regime may achieve the same social goals but by different means. Instead of direct supply of services by the state, the same and potentially better services can now be supplied by private actors who are regulated by state institutions. The state is not on the retreat, its regulatory machine is stronger than ever, and the new regimes of "ordered competition" may ensure that the regulatory state may continue to be also a "positive state".

A historical perspective on the politics of change is offered through the study of the sixteen regimes for the governance of telecom and electricity since the very beginning of their commercialization (about 1880). The historical development of these industries in the United States and the United Kingdom is contrasted for the last 120 years. These two networks are ideal for comparison (to the extent that we can achieve our ideals) not only because they have developed in the same historical period, but also because they enjoy some common important characteristics. They are both important public services; they have characteristics of natural monopolies; they are network industries (organized around grids - which critically determine their natural monopoly characteristics); and they have similar life cycles in terms of ownership and competition. Variations in the extent of technological innovations that have fostered incentive for regulatory reforms, in the two networks, provide evidence of the political nature of the changes and demonstrate its comprehensiveness.

The two countries studied here belong to the "Anglo-Saxon" type of polity and policy making. They are commonly characterized as one of the same type of state: early industrialist, pluralist, liberal, or weak. But as will become evident immediately, their approach to the governance of telecom and electricity have differed remarkably since the

1880s. The British were quick to exert tight political control over telecom and electricity, and later moved to create first a mixture of public-private regime and then to nationalize the industries. The Americans, by contrast, took steps to control the two industries in an effective way on the federal level only in the mid-1930s, and in doing so they generally eschewed public ownership and put their trust in the regulation of private monopolies. Since the 1980s both the British and the Americans have moved towards what may be termed ordered competition and the consolidation of the "Competition State". Through various and complex strategies of regulation, deregulation, reregulation, privatization, and liberalization they created another layer of state institutions which was embedded in the old structures of the state.

The paper starts with analytical distinctions of several ideal types of governance regimes for telecom and electricity. These distinctions help in distinguishing strategies and structures and in differentiating sixteen different regimes for the governance of telecom and electricity in the US and Britain. The second part of the paper presents a comparative analysis of the dynamics of change in the US and the UK. It deals with the structures (regimes) rather than the sources of change in its aim to conceptualize the dynamics of change in these two countries rather than to explain why they happened. The third part of the paper is an examination of the dynamics of social and economic intervention in the two countries and in the different regimes. The fourth part addresses the rise of competition state and presents some of its highly interventionist characteristics. The process that leads towards convergence in the "competition state" in the US and the UK, it is argued, concurs with the creation of new divergencies with effects that are still less eye-catching than those of convergence (on these new divergencies, see Eberlein's paper in this volume).

I. Governance Regimes for Telecom and Electricity

Governance regimes are structures that reflect a sticky (and therefore stable) political, economic, and technological order, sustained by political norms and institutions and a certain balance of power in the sector's policy community. A sectoral regime, such as that for telecom and electricity, may exist on various levels of governance, for instance, the municipal, regional, national, and international. The sectoral regime itself is an amalgamation of "micro-regimes" that govern different aspects of the sector. For example, the electricity regime may be an amalgamation of the regimes for generation (production of electricity by generators), transmission (the transport of electricity over high-voltage grids for long distance), distribution (the diffusion to clients), and interconnection (the economic and technical terms for connecting different grids). Likewise, the telecom regime may include different micro-regimes for foreign investment, equipment, interconnection of networks, international telephony, etc. The extent of state control, ownership, or competition in one part of the sector or micro-regime (e.g., generation, international telephony) is not necessarily the same as in the other parts of the sector (e.g., distribution). Sectoral regimes are autonomous entities with rules, institutions and policy communities of their own. Their autonomy however does not mean that they are independent: they are affected by (and they affect) more general, economic, legal, political regimes on both the national and international levels.

Below, some ideal types of liberal, social, and etatist regimes are presented. Table 1 presents ideal types of municipal regimes for both telecom and electricity and helps to distinguish national from municipal (and regional) regimes. The municipal regimes are characterized by municipal control over critical issues such as digging the streets and erecting electricity and telecom poles. They are also characterized by municipal control over the granting of franchises and the determination of the terms of these franchises. Municipal control can be a matter of local decision, based on common law, or grounded, like in the British Electricity Supply Acts of 1882 and 1888, in national legislation. These regimes may take one of two forms, social or liberal, depending on the patterns of ownership, the terms of the franchises, and the extent to which a monopoly is grounded in law. The table presents the "ideal types" of social and liberal regimes, and in fact one finds a mixture of social and liberal micro-regimes especially in Britain, where debates over the desired regimes for telecom and especially electricity went on for decades.

Table 1: Not all Telecom and Electricity Regimes are National Regimes

Social-Municipal Telecom Regime	**Social-Municipal Electricity Regime**	**Liberal-Municipal Telecom regime**	**Liberal-Municipal Electricity Regime**
Franchise and right-of-way are controlled by the municipality. The municipality has the monopoly over the supply of telecom services.	Distribution, generation and transmission (to the extent that it is developed) are all in the hands of the municipality, which also controls the franchises and right-of-way	The municipality controls franchises and right-of way. It transfers them to profit-motivated companies. Franchises are usually long-term (over 20 years) & right-of-way is guaranteed to the holders of the franchises.	Franchises and right-of-way are in the hands of the municipality, which transfers them to profit-companies. Franchises are usually long-term (over 30 years) & right-of-way is guaranteed to the holders of the franchises.

Some traces of municipal and regional regimes for the governance of telecom and electricity exist even today (more in electricity than in telephone). However, towards the mid-1890s in telephony and the 1920s in electricity, organization on larger scale gradually created regimes on larger scale, and notably pushed towards the creation of national and international regimes for telecommunications. Although both telephony and electricity are network industries, telecom as a "two-way" network is different from the "one-way" electricity network. The value of the telephone network for each user grows in direct proportion for the number of subscribers to the networks and its geographical spread. This is not the case in electricity, where the consumption of electricity by a user is not necessarily dependent on the number of other consumers (although more electricity consumers may improve the terms - tariffs and reliability - of all consumers).

The creation of national regimes for telecom and electricity led to the creation of two types of regimes, etatist and liberal. In the case of telecom, etatism was reflected in a very strict state control over the supply of telecom, but more importantly in the transfer of the responsibility for the provision of services to the hands of the state. In many cases, and most definitely in Europe, this led to the creation of the Post-Telegraph-Telephony complex (PTT), where one ministry was responsible for the provision of all these services (Noam, 1992). In the case of electricity, similar phenomena occurred, although the provision of services was usually a matter for a state corporation rather than a ministry. The alternative to the etatist regime was the liberal regime of private regulated monopoly. The distinction between the two was not in the extent of competition but in the form of ownership. In liberal regimes telecom was under private ownership, so the provision of services, which was a matter for private ownership, was clearly distinguished from the roles of regulation and policy making, which were the domain of the state. The geographical scope of the monopoly varied in such regimes and across the two sectors. In some countries there was one company that dealt with all forms of telecom and electricity supply, in others there were a few companies that had regional spheres of provision with de facto or legal demarcation lines.

Table 2: Not all Monopolistic Regimes are Etatist

Etatist Telecom Regimes	Etatist Electricity Regimes	Liberal-National Telecom regimes of private-regulated monopoly	Liberal-National Electricity Regimes of private-regulated monopoly
Franchises & rights-of-way are governed by the state. Telecom services are provided by the state. Policy making, regulatory functions and ownership are in the hands of one state agency.	Distribution, generation, and transmission are all in the hands of the state. Special laws explicitly express the monopoly of the state in this sphere, covering franchises and rights-of-way also.	Franchises and rights-of way are under state control. These rights are transferred to profit- motivated companies. Franchises are usually long-term (over 20 years) & rights-of-way are guaranteed to the holders of the franchises.	Franchises and rights-of way are under state control. These rights are transferred to profit- motivated companies. Franchises are usually long-term (over 20 years) & right-of-way is guaranteed to the holders of the franchises.

While monopoly was the common form of organization, the extent of regionalism differed between telecom and electricity. Telecom has more national and international features and is organized across a much larger geographical range than electricity. In fact, telecom is the first technology to require an international form of governance. As early as 1865 the provision of telegraph and telephone calls across borders made it necessary to create the International Telegraph Union (ITU, today the), which is the oldest existing international institution.[1] Liberal-national regimes for the provision of telecom and electricity were characterized between the 1930s and the 1980s by private ownership on the one hand and the regulatory role as the dominant role of government (planning and ownership were much less important public goals than the regulation of tariffs and services). While the government took control over franchise and right-of-way from municipalities and regional bodies (and in the US, from the states), it supported and even promoted the private provision of these services.

Since the late 1970s the terms of liberal telecom and electricity regime have acquired new meaning. Liberalism has come to be identified not only with private ownership but also with the promotion of competition in these industries, which had been widely perceived as natural monopolies. The introduction of competition to the telecom and electricity regime created two forms of liberal regimes, laissez-faire and "ordered competition". The laissez-faire regime emphasizes minimum regulation (strategy of deregulation) and reliance on general laws of competition. The regime of "ordered competition" emphasizes the creation of regulatory structures that will maximize competition (economic re-regulation) through the creation of regulatory regimes that actively promote competition. Unlike the protection of competition, practiced by laissez-faire-oriented regimes, the regime of ordered competition actively promotes competition. In addition, unlike the laissez-faire regime, which leaves the maximization of social welfare to the market, the regime of ordered competition creates industry-specific balances between economic and social goals through social regulation of private activities (rather than public ownership).

These ideal types of telecom and electricity regime allow us to present in the next part of this paper the dynamics of change in the American and British telecom and electricity regimes.

An international organization of electricity generation, World Power Conference, was established only in 1924. The organizational development of this organization was very slow (its primary action was to hold international conference every three years). It is now called the World Energy Council.

Table 3: Not all "For Competition" Regimes are "Laissez-Faire" Regimes

Laissez-faire Telecom Regime	Laissez-faire Electricity Regime	Telecom Regime of Ordered Competition	Electricity Regime of Ordered Competition
Privatization and deregulation of telecom networks and airways. Entry and exit are matters for economic decision making by private entities. General competition laws are applied to the sector. Public policy making and public regulation have minimal role in the function of the network.	Privatization and deregulation of generation, distribution, and transmission grids. Entry and exit are matters for economic decision making by private entities. General competition laws are applied to the sector. Public policy making and public regulation have minimal role in the function of the network.	Sector-specific rules and independent regulatory agency. The major aim is the promotion of competition through the arrangement and enforcement of interconnection agreements and numbering schemes. High discretion of the regulatory agency including the option of asymmetrical regulation. The regime is carefully designed to accommodate economic and social regulation	Sector-specific rules and independent regulatory agency. The major aim is the promotion of competition through the arrangement and enforcement of open and equal access to the grids. High discretion of the regulatory agency including the option of asymmetrical regulation. The regime is carefully designed to accommodate economic and social regulation

II. REGIME CHANGE IN THE GOVERNANCE OF BRITISH AND AMERICAN TELECOM AND ELECTRICITY

Different trajectories of governance are clearly evident in Britain and the United States. This part of the paper offers historical perspective on the dynamics of governance, which allow us to understand better both continuity and change. It serves to portray the British case as a change from a Service-provision state to a Competition state and the American case as a change from a Regulatory State to a Competition state.

The Municipal Regimes

The first regimes for the governance of telephony and electricity were municipal both in the United States and in Britain (see table 4). The power to grant franchises to erect poles and to determine their conditions was in the hands of municipalities. Internal disputes within the British state, in particular between local and central government, over the control of these systems resulted in restrictive policies towards the private operators of telephony and electricity. Such policies resulted in a slower diffusion of telephony and electricity than in the United States, where the political climate was much warmer towards telephone and electricity companies. For example, when Thomas Edison pursued a franchise to lay the distribution system for the first electricity supply station in Pearl Street New York City, he hired a special train that brought the mayor and the aldermen to his laboratory in Menlo Park. The extravagant electricity display that he organized helped to persuade the council to grant the concession despite objections of gaslight and lamplighters interests (Hughes, 1983, 30). Frequently electricity and telephone companies had to deal with corrupt officials at the local municipality (see, for example, Insull's experience with the "Gray Wolves: Anderson, 1981, 34) but despite these obstacles private for-profit telecom and electricity companies had a favorable political environment.

Table 4: The Dynamics of Telecom and Electricity Regimes in the US and the UK

Telecom		Electricity	
US	**UK**	**US**	**UK**
1878-1907 Municipal Liberal Regulatory Regime	1879-1896 Liberal Regime with Restrictive Regulation by both the Municipalities and the State	1882-1907: Municipal Liberal Regulatory Regime	1882-1919: Social-Liberal Municipal Regime
1907-1934 State Regulatory Regime of Private Monopoly (dual service competition; 1894 to 1924)	1896-1911 Hybrid regime of mixed ownership and restrictive competition	1907-1935 State-regulatory regime of Private Monopolies and limited Competition	1919-1948 The National Regime of Mixed Ownership and Restrictive Regulation
1934-1984 Federal Regulatory Regime of Private Monopoly Regime and very limited competition	1911-1982 The Etatist Regime (Post, Telegraph and Telephony Industrial Complex)	1935-1992: Federal-State Regime of Regulate Private Monopolies	1948-1983 The Etatist Regime
1984-1996 Private Regulated Monopoly with Limited Competition	1982-1997 Private Regulated duopoly with Limited Competition	1979-1992 Regime of Private Regulated Monopolies with very limited Competition	1983 –1989 Regime of Private Regulated Monopolies with very limited Competition
1996- Regime of Ordered Competition	1997 - Regime of Ordered Competition	1992- Regime of Ordered Competition	1989 – Regime of Ordered Competition

By contrast, the British tended to see telecom and electricity as legitimate spheres for public action. When the Bell and Edison telephone companies established the United Telephone Company in 1880 to offer telephone services in London, the government (the Post & Telegraph authorities, The Postmaster General) went to court and argued that it was the exclusive right of the state to offer telephone services.[2] When the court decided in favor of the government, but it was clear that neither the Parliament nor the Treasury would allow the Postmaster General to invest in telephone communication, a compromise was reached. The Postmaster General granted the company a license for the provision of telephony in exchange for waiving its right to appeal the court decision, and a royalty payment of 10%. This was not an isolated event. A similar pattern of early politicization in Britain is evident in electricity. So quick was the British Parliament to move to examine the subject that already in 1879, few years before electricity was first offered on commercial basis, a parliamentary committee studied the subject (Poulter, 1986, 26-27). The first Electricity Lighting Act, most probably the first of its type in the world, soon followed in 1882.

Differences in political climates between Britain and the US were followed by divergent approaches towards ownership rights. In 1889 the municipality of Bradford became the first municipal authority in Britain to open its own electricity supply station (Poulter, 1986, 27). By 1900 more than 50% of the 250 suppliers were owned by municipalities. Municipal ownership was widespread in the United States also (Schap, 1986, 9-10). But the American municipal undertakings were on a much smaller scale than their private competitors, and they were "dwarfed by the major urban systems controlled by Edison companies and other investor-owned utilities" (Hannah, 1979b, 578). By 1902, when 815 municipal systems had been already formed, their combined capacity accounted for only 9.3% of the total (Hirsh, 1989, 22).

Municipal ownership in electricity was a stronger and a more widespread phenomenon than in telephony all over the world. Yet, the forces of municipal socialism in the 1890s were so strong in Britain that even in the case of telephony there were considerable political efforts not only to protect the regulative powers of the municipalities but also to promote municipal ownership. Under considerable pressure and with widespread political support by the press, a law authorizing localities to open their own telephone exchanges was approved by the parliament (The 1899 Telegraph Act) (Meyer, 1907, 7). This effort was an utter failure and the only current evidence of its impact is the municipal telephone exchange of Hull. Yet the existence of the Hull exchange reflects more the failure of British municipal socialism in telephony than its vitality.[3] The British effort to create social-municipal telephone regime is especially puzzling since the telephone was a luxury back then (unlike electricity). Moreover, with the development of long-distance technology, networks transcended the local boundaries

---

[2] The first public telephone exchange in America was opened in New Haven in 1878. The first in Britain was opened in London a year later.

[3] Municipal ownership of the telephone was much more successful in the Netherlands and Canada. In the United States there were only a few scattered systems, the largest and the most successful begin that of Brookings, South Dakota (Glaeser, 1957, 446).

and acquired regional and national scope so technology and economy did not support functional organization on the basis of municipal boundaries. Municipal ownership of telephony was a rarity in the United States as well (Schiller, 1998, 402; Glaeser, 1957, 446). With the exception of British electricity, the municipal regimes were based on the power of municipalities to regulate wayleaves rather than on public ownership.

Away from Municipalism: The New British and American Regimes

While municipal ownership of electricity supply continued to be a widespread phenomenon in the UK, political governance structures were transformed to higher political levels. This happened in British telephony around 1896 and in electricity after World War I. In telephony, the process started with a move by the British government in 1892 to acquire the long-distance lines of the private National Telephone Company. Negotiations with the company on purchase terms and on the relations between local and long-distance telephony continued for more than three years, and only in 1896 did the Post Office become the de facto provider of long- distance services. While the new regime did not give new regulatory powers to the government it made it a critical player in the field of telephone supply. As before, local authorities retained their right to veto wayleaves; and as before, they often used their rights in a way that obstructed the spread of the technology (Meyer, 1907, 57). It is interesting to note that these early moves to state ownership and the creation of a national telephone regime in Britain were not followed by any corresponding regime change in the United States. Instead, that country evinced interesting internal changes, which resulted in growth of competition to an extent and scope not observed elsewhere in the world up until the 1990s (see Mueller, 1997; Bickers, 1991).

A movement away from municipalism is observable also in the British electricity regime. The necessity of some form of national coordination was already fairly evident in the 19th century for the country to enjoy the benefits of economics of scale. But it was politically very difficult to establish control over the hundreds of electricity undertakings of the municipalities on the one hand and the private suppliers on the other. The Electricity Act of 1919 established a national regulatory regime with a limited coordinating role for the government in ownership and development of the national high-voltage transmission network. In addition, the Act established the Office of Electricity Commissioners, who were supposed to promote voluntary agreements between electricity suppliers to ensure the economic benefits of large-scale generation. The failure of the electricity commissioners in this led in 1926 to a new legislation that created a public corporation, the Electricity Board, which took over the development and ownership of the high-voltage grid (Hannah, 1979a). In addition, a national coordination system of generation was established, putting into service the most efficient generators and thus achieving efficiency on the national level.

The Consolidation of State-level Regulatory Regimes in the US

Regulatory structures for the governance of American telephony and electricity started to evolve rapidly from 1907 on state level. Before 1907, eight states regulated the telephone. Forty-two states and the District of Columbia had regulated telephony by 1920 (Cohen, 1991, 57). A similar process, in the same period, was observable also in the field of electricity. As with telephony, A few states created a regulatory regime for electricity relatively early (in 1887 Massachusetts had extended the power of its Board of Gas Commissioners to include electric lighting). But the turning point came in 1907, when New York, and shortly afterwards Wisconsin, created the prototypes of the modern public service commission (McCraw, 1971, 13). By 1913, the total number of states that had their own regulatory commissions was 29 (Anderson, 1981, 56). Since 1910 there were also considerable attempts to move telecom and electricity regulation to the federal level. Yet despite the weakness of the state-level regime these efforts ended up with very limited results. In the case of telephony, an amendment to the Mann-Elkins bill (1910) which originally was intended to regulate only railways, transferred interstate telephone traffic to the jurisdiction of the Interstate Commerce Commission (ICC). In 1921, Congress gave the ICC the power to oversee mergers and acquisitions of telephone companies (Cohen, 1991, 63-4). Still, the ICC contribution to the institutionalization of effective regulatory regime at the federal level was marginal (Gabel, 1969, 357). In 1913 the Justice Department filed suit against AT&T and compelled the company to offer the "Kingsbury commitment". Under this commitment AT&T was obliged to dispose of its interests in Western Union Telegraph, to stop the practice of purchasing its competitors, and to allow interconnection of competitors' networks to its own network (Brooks, 1975, 132-7).

In the sphere of electricity the first major move toward federal regulation was in the sphere of hydroelectric schemes. In 1920 Congress passed the Federal Water Power Act that gave an ex-officio commission[4] the authority to set the terms for the use of such sources for the public benefit (Glaeser, 1957, 148-9). In 1927 the Supreme Court held that state authority to regulate electric rates was limited to matters of local distribution, thus implying that federal regulation was required for moving electric energy across state lines (Glaeser, 1957, 149; Berlin et al., 1974, 53). These early indications of some functional need to transfer authority to a higher level of governance were not acted on until the crisis of the great depression and the New Deal.

In contrast to the considerable variation between telecom and electricity in Britain, the American regimes presented much more coherent patterns of development. The American approach to ownership was similar for both telecom and electricity. Their shift from municipal to state-level governance, as well as the early signs of federal-level regulations, all reflected a similar approach and appeared almost concurrently. The British, however, at that time, adopted a different approach to the governance of telecom and electricity. An early significant move was the nationalization of the long-distance telephony network in 1896, and then the creation of an etatist regime with the

[4] Comprising the Secretary of War as chairman, the Secretary of the Interior and the Secretary of Agriculture.

nationalization of the entire telephony network in 1911. This led to the birth of the Post, Telegraph, and Telephony complex, which dominated the British communications regime for more than 70 years and for most of the telephone era (Noam, 1992, 103-132). True, the Americans experienced nationalization of the telephone network as well. In 1918 the progressive administration of Wilson presented a bill for the nationalization of the telephone and telegraph systems. Congress unenthusiastically approved it, but a year later, when telephone rates were raised by the government, it passed a joint resolution requiring the telegraph and telephone administration to be return to private control (Bickers, 1991, 90-1).

The Federal Regimes for Telecom and Electricity

The 1930s were a critical period in the development of the American regimes, as regulatory structures at the Federal level for both telecom and electricity were constructed. These regimes were on one hand highly regulated: industry was subject to strict rate, service, and merger and acquisition regulations. On the other hand, they served to legitimate the private monopoly of telecom and electricity supply. The new telephone regime was institutionalized by the Federal Communications Act of 1934, which created the Federal Communications Commission with authority over the regulation of interstate telecommunications. The act only consolidated various laws in the hands of one authority (the FCC), which since then has served as the locus of state authority in the field of communications. The FCC however did not replace the states' utility commissions and thus a two-level regulatory structure was institutionalized.

Similar developments are observable in electricity, although unlike telecom, the creation of a federal regime for electricity was the grounds for one of the most extensive battles between progressives and conservatives (McCraw, 1971; Anderson, 1981). The new regime had two main components. The first was the federal regulatory structure that was imposed on investors-owned electricity suppliers, and the other included the promotion of electricity schemes (primarily the development of hydro-power resources, and also the diffusion of electricity to rural areas). The most dynamic component of this regime seemed to be the large-scale hydroelectric and irrigation scheme promoted by the Tennessee Valley Authority from the second half of the 1930s. However, by the early 1950s it had become clear that government entrepreneurship in hydroelectric projects in particular, and in electricity in general, was stagnating; hence, regulation again came to be perceived as the most important component of the regime.

In 1930 Congress institutionalized the ex-officio Federal Power Commission that had been established in 1920 by giving it concrete a organizational structure to be run by five commissioners. But it was only in 1935 that an effective and comprehensive federal regulatory regime was created. The Federal Power Act of that year expanded the jurisdiction of the Federal Power Commission by giving it power to regulate the rates and service of electric and natural gas utilities when the transactions were in interstate commerce (in addition to federal hydroelectric power). The commission was also given control over national defense issues, accounting, and consolidations of electric utilities. In addition it was empowered to make special investigations of electricity rates and interstate transmission of electricity (Glaeser, 1957, 149-150). The 1933 Securities and Exchange Commission Act and the 1935 Public Utility Holding Company Act further strengthened the federal regulatory regime. These acts governed particular aspects of the finance (debt and equity capital) of the electricity utilities and their organizational structure (mergers and acquisitions) (Berlin et al., 1974, 80). Like the Federal telecom regime, the federal electricity regime is a two-level regime where there is (often uneasy) division of labor between the federal regulatory structure and the state-level structure.

The second component of the electricity regime is based on promotional policies. The Rural Electrification Administration order of 1935 and the Rural Electrification Administration Act of 1936 created an extensive program of rural electrification (Clayton, 1980). Rural electrification programs were supported by state entrepreneurship. The most important program, economically and symbolically, was the creation of the Tennessee Valley Authority in 1933. While its establishment was justified on grounds of flood control, job creation, and rural development, its central objective from the outset was to supply electricity for consumers cooperatives in rural areas (Brennan et al., 1996, 24). In 1937 the Bonneville Power Administration was created to coordinate the supply of hydroelectric power generation from Columbia River system. The dynamic development of this component of the American electricity regime stagnated in the post-war period. In 1950s, the heyday of electricity nationalization all over the world, President Eisenhower suggested that the TVA should be privatized. While, the suggestion was rejected by Congress, eagerness for direct state development projects was no longer visible. The basic structure was however stable, with few only few modifications that did not change this basic structure. In 1954 the Atomic Energy Act created the Atomic Energy Commission, with a dual role as promoter and regulator of nuclear power (Berlin et al., 1974, 83). In addition, after the Northeast blackout of 1965, utilities began forming regional coordination mechanisms to improve to reliability of supply. In 1968 the National Electric Reliability Council (NERC) was formed as a self-governed organization of the Utilities, but with the non-voting right of participation by federal and state-level commissioners (Berlin et al., 1974, 73-4).

Convergence on Etatism - The British Telecom and Electricity Regimes

From about 1911 and until 1947 the British had two distinct governance regimes for telecom and electricity. While the state Postmaster General was the exclusive provider of telecommunications in Britain (international communications was supplied by Cable & Wireless), private and municipal undertakings were the dominant suppliers of electricity. True, since1926 the state had been the owner of the electricity transmission grid and played an important coordination role, but the difference from the state monopoly over telecom was significant. The Electricity Act of 1947 eliminated the sectoral differences. Responsibility for electricity generation and high-voltage transmission was transferred to the government while distribution was assigned to regional electricity authorities which were owned by the government; this represented a transfer of ownership from the municipal to the national level. At the center of the etatist regime stood the Central Electricity Generation Board, a public corporation, which in addition to the transmission network also controlled all the generation facilities. Never before in the history of British electricity had such a concentration of power to decide and implement existed in one institution.[5] A web of forces that seemed invincible supported these etatist regimes, which endured intact until 1980s with little sign of change. Public managers, labor unions, and court-suppliers of equipment stood at the center of what may be called the electricity/telecom industrial complex.

The Provisional Telecom and Electricity Regimes of the 1980s

From the end of the 1970s and throughout the 1980s the telecom and electricity regimes in both the US and the UK experienced significant pressures for change, which resulted in the creation of provisional regimes that lasted about a decade. Compared with the old regimes, they were more liberal. They were for promoting radical privatization plans (telecom and electricity in the UK); reducing entry barriers (telecom and electricity in both countries) and enforcing divestiture of the dominant players (AT&T, and later, in Britain, the Central Electricity Generation Board). The first change is observable in the American electricity regime, which became subject to the new federal legislation of the Public Utilities Regulatory Policies Act (1978).[6] The act created a category of private electricity suppliers that were exempted from rate regulation. The private regulated utilities were *obliged* to purchase electricity from these new independent suppliers (Gilbert and Kahn, 1996, 199-200). The terms of the transactions were left largely to the discretion of state-level commissions that could determine the price at a level that did not exceed the avoided costs[7] of new capacity (Brennan et al., 1996, 29). Important provisions of the new regime were aimed at reducing uncertainties for new entrants that derived from the economic power of the incumbent operators. These provisions made sure that new entrants would get attractive prices for their electricity. The success of the regime in encouraging new entry was remarkable: by 1991 independent power accounted for almost 9% of all electricity sales (Gilbert and Kahn, 1996, 204). Their share in new generation capacity grew from 20% in 1986 to over 60% in 1994 (Brennan et al., 1996, 30).

Similar provisions to encourage new generators were made also by the designers of the new electricity regime in Britain, which was created by the 1983 Energy Act. The Act removed statutory constraints on the entry of private generation companies and required the regional distribution boards to purchase their electricity from the cheapest available source and at prices based on their avoided costs. However, while the goals of this regime

5 The new statist order of the post war period became even more monolithic with the nationalization of the Imperial telecommunications provider Cable & Wireless [1947].

6 The extent of transformation in comparison to the old regime was not radical and smaller then the Carter's administration was hoping for.

7 Avoided costs were calculated as the price that the utility would save by not having to build new plants to provide what they could get from the independent generator.

were similar to those of the 1978 American regime, the outcomes, in terms of newly independent competitors, were disappointing (OECD, 1997, 218). Somewhat similar disappointing results were experienced in the British telecommunications, although in this case a more radical move was carried out. While the British government hesitated to privatize electricity, in 1981 it moved to privatize Cable & Wireless, and in 1984 to privatize 51% of British Telecom (the remaining public stake was sold in 1990 and 1993) (Thatcher, 1999, 94). The privatization of British Telecom was accompanied by the establishment of the Office of Telecommunications (OFTEL) and the nomination of an industry watchdog, the Director General of Telecommunications. In keeping with a new "duopoly policy", an additional national telecom provider, Mercury Communications, was licensed in 1982. The monopoly over terminal equipment was terminated (with the exclusion of the first telephone set) and so was the monopoly over the value-added services. The new regime, however, avoided the divestiture of British Telecom, declined to accept recommendation to open British Telecom to third parties, and committed itself to a restrictive licensing regime until 1990 (Hulsink, 1999).

The divestiture of AT&T in 1984 is one of the most notable achievement of antitrust laws in the US and elsewhere. To some extent it reflects the most critical landmarks in the changing of the world's telecom regimes. Yet this "earthquake" event was less ambitious in the restructuring of the telecom regime than the regime that followed it about a decade later. The divestiture of AT&T was aimed at increasing the competition in the long-distance market for telephony, which was perceived by the Department of Justice as potentially competitive.[8] The decree was signed in 1982 and originated from an antitrust suit filed already in 1974 and implemented in 1984. It radically transformed the structure of the American telecom market without transforming the legal foundations and the governance structure itself. By 1984 AT&T's vertical ownership was restructured, and the company had to give up its 22 local monopoly companies. By radically separating the long-distance arm of AT&T from the local services, the decree aimed at ensuring that AT&T would no longer be able to place obstacles before competition in long-distance telephony. The local monopolies were required to provide access "equal in type, quality and price" to all long-distance companies.

Regimes of Ordered Competition for Telecom and Electricity

In the 1990s The British and American regimes for electricity and telecom moved towards a significantly more pro-competitive structure. These new regimes, which still have to be consolidated, are aimed at restructuring generation, transmission, distribution, and supply of electricity. In addition, they seek the creation of choice among electricity suppliers for both businesses and private consumers of electricity. This implies extensive restructuring of the sector, far more ambitious than the goal of competition in generation that characterized the proceeding regime. Similarly in telecom, competition goals were

[8] The consent decree was a court modified agreement between the antirust authorities in the Department of Justice and AT&T.

extended from the equipment and long-distance markets to local telephony while opening the telephone markets to cable companies (and vice versa) and the long-distance market to local telephony providers (and vice versa). Competition rules have been devised for virtually all parts of the telephony and electricity sector, with growing sophistication of the regulatory regimes compared with the past.

A move towards the creation of a regime of ordered competition was first observable in British electricity. In 1989 a White Paper on electricity privatization led to a new electricity act, which promoted a far-reaching plan for restructuring the industry (Thomas, 1996). While in telecom (1984) and gas (1986) privatization was the major feature of the change, in electricity it went much farther. The proposals of the White Paper were aimed at changing the rules of the game and at structuring the market. The Central Electricity Generation Board was divided into four parts: two fossil-fueled generators (PowerGen and National Power), one nuclear power generator (Nuclear Electric) and one high-tension transmission company (National Grid). The 12 local distribution companies in England and Wales, now to be known as Regional Electricity Companies (RECs), were privatized at the end of 1990.[9] By mid-1991 the system had been completely transformed, undergoing the most radical restructuring since nationalization at 1947. At the center of the new regime stood a new regulatory agency, the Office of Electricity Regulation, a watchdog that enjoyed wide authority in respect of the natural monopolists in transmission and distribution. The duties of regulator included both the promotion of competition and the protection of consumers. Consumer freedom to choose suppliers was extended gradually, starting first with the large business consumers, next moving to a category of medium-level consumers, and finally to include households and other small consumers (Newbery and Green 1996). The central element of this micro-regime, which ensured the freedom to chose a supplier, was the obligation of the natural monopolists to transfer electricity from any source and upon demand of the customer at prices and conditions closely monitored by the regulator.

The creation of a regime of ordered competition in the US by the 1992 Energy Policy Act gave the Federal Energy Regulatory Commission (FERC) new powers. The FERC had the power to determine the terms of access to the transmission grid and to force transmission-owning utilities to deliver power at reasonable, non-discriminatory, and cost-based rates. In April 1996 the FERC issued guidelines and procedures for implementation. The act, however, did not impose competition, and left much discretion in the hands of the state commissions. The result is a bottom-up approach for the creation of a competitive regime, in which some states have led the way and are moving fast to create state-level regimes of ordered competition, while others are taking a much more passive approach. However, the option of bypassing the utilities network by self-generation and co-generation is becoming increasingly realistic and creates incentives for an America-wide regime of ordered competition (Gilbert and Kahn, 1994, 197). Action

[9] The Scottish system and North Irish electrical system were privatized according to different models. However, the English and Welsh electricity included about 88% of the total so it is justified to characterize the British trajectory according to the governance regime of England and Wales (Thomas, 1996, 47).

by Congress may well be necessary to implement full retail competition (Brennan et al., 1996, 7-8).

The creation of a British regime of ordered regulation advanced very slowly. Unlike the "big bangs" of electricity restructuring, the privatization of BT and even the American Telecom Act of 1996, the movement towards a regime of "ordered competition" was critically a matter for the discretion of the regulator, the Director General for Telecommunications. This was so even though the British Telecom Act of 1984 does not specifically make it the duty of the regulator to promote competition (Prosser, 1997, 74). Signs of change towards the extension of competition from customer equipment, value added services, and duopoly to a more comprehensive conception of competition came with the duopoly review of 1991 (Thatcher, 1994). In consequence, the regulator encouraged cable television companies and other potential competitors to provide telecom services in direct competition with BT. A system of asymmetric regulation was constructed. British Telecom was subjected to levies such as the access deficit contribution, and was prohibited from providing video services. At the same time, the new entrants were exempted from both the levy and the prohibition of joint provision of telephone and video (Collins and Murroni, 1996, 475-6). The point of no return in the institutionalization of the new regime was the setting of rules for the interconnection of micro-regimes, which were announced in March 1994 (Prosser, 1997, 75). However, only in July 1997 were the final proposals for interconnection regime set, to be effective from October 1997 (only a few months before the final date set by the EU Interconnection Dirctive). The interconnection regime allowed the subscribers of new entrants to connect with the network of the incumbent, thereby establishing the economic and technical terms for effective competition. Without an interconnection regime, and considerable regulatory safeguards, competition will be much less feasible; therefore, interconnection should be conceived as a central component of the newly created regime of ordered competition.

The American regime of ordered competition in telecom was created by the 1996 Telecom Act. While the former (provisional) regime created the conditions for limited long-distance competition between long-distance telephone operators, it retained the local monopolies of Baby Bells. The local operators were prohibited from providing long-distance telephony, and the long-distance operators were prohibited from providing local telephony. In addition, the old regime restricted competition by prohibiting entry of the Baby Bells into the equipment market and making it impossible for telephone operators to own cable networks. While all these prohibitions were fixed at the time in order to make a level playing field for competition, in the 1990s they came to be perceived as outdated. The Telecom Act of 1996, passed by a Republican-dominated Congress, formulated the general rules for communication-wide competition. The new act, which replaced the 1934 legislation, covers several hundred pages and should be perceived, despite the deregulatory rhetoric, as a true manifestation of the positive-sum relations between regulation and competition in regimes of ordered competition. Not only does the legislation favor more competition with more rules (cf. Vogel, 1996) but it is "the FCC's task to ensure that interconnection, service and network element prices developed by the established [telecommunications operators] are just and reasonable, non-discriminatory, and fashioned without resort to cross-subsidization" (Bolter, 1996, 453). How far the new regime relied on regulations became even clearer when the FCC issued its regulation in August 1996. They included not less than 668 pages of guidelines! (Curwen, 1997, 177). A significant place in these guidelines is accorded to the interconnection regime. The provisions in this regard are currently being challenged in court, and it will take a number of years more until actual competition in the local loop will become effective.

III. THE REGULATORY STATE AS A POSITIVE STATE

The analysis of the telecom and electricity regimes in the two countries may serve to identify the social implications of the different state trajectories in the last century. Especially important are the questions of whether British etatism until the 1980s was socially superior to the American regulatory regime of private monopoly; and whether today's convergence on ordered competition implies a decline in the positivism of these states. Starting with the old regimes, it seems that despite nationalization of telecom and electricity in Britain, and despite the more protective political culture of the British (than the Americans), neither telephony nor electricity were supplied for free, or even below cost. On the contrary, electricity consumers subsidized coal and nuclear energy, and often telephony revenues were used to subsidize the post. In fact, the rationale for the nationalization of these services in Britain and for their regulation in America was only marginally their diffusion for the poor and/or periphery. More important were the issues of tariffs and service control for *all* users. State provision of telecom and electricity sometimes implied tariff reduction, but not necessarily, and at times public ownership is inferior both economically and socially. In addition, the advantages and disadvantages of regulation versus public ownership should not be a matter for static policy calculations but should be seen in dynamic terms and from a historical perspective. Rural electrification has proceeded extremely slowly in the United States, compared with Europe, for half a century (Nye, 1990, 287). Only with the state entrepreneurial activity in the form of the Rural Electricity Administration was a breakthrough possible (Fischer, 1992, 258). It seems very convincing that the private regime of electricity provision in America in that period was socially inferior to the European, yet this does not imply directly that one should continue to support rural electrification by state agency nowadays.

Moreover, while the American welfare state indeed lags behind the British, it enjoys some advantages in telecom and electricity that reflect on the social value of regulatory regimes, particularly the ability of these regimes to balance social and economic regulations. For example, in telephony the American regime allowed cross-subsidies between long-distance and local services, and even between different states, in order to promote general coverage and affordable telephone rates (Blau, 1997, 249). In electricity, in the setting of the 1970s energy crises many states institutionalized sector-specific subsidies for low-income households (Anderson, 1981, 135-165). Similar programs were devised in the 1980s for telephony to offer low monthly subscription rates (in some places, as low as $1.00 per month for limited local service). The Link-Up American program waived telephony deposit fees and allowed payments for connection charges to be spread out over long periods (Blau, 1997, 250). The life-line programs made special subsidies available to many households; the limits on their growth were not policy deficiencies of regulation as a mode of governance but political opposition by conservatives and capitalists.

The issue of universal service is highly illuminating in this regard. The terminology of universal service originated in the United States and reflects some contradictory notions. In the beginning of the 20th century it was used by Theodore Vail, the architect of the AT&T hegemonic telephone order in America, to justify the existence of one public telephone network that would connect all users (Mueller, 1997, 8). In the post-war period the notion of Universal Service acquired a new social meaning which was broader than Vail's notion. It meant that telephone services should be offered on an affordable basis to all Americans. Examining British notions of post-war access to the telephone, Hills found that compared with social welfare, education or health, over which until the 1980s there was a post-war consensus in favor of provision on a universal basis, no such consensus has existed in telecommunications (Hills, 1989). While one may argue that telecom services are less socially critical than health services, unemployment benefits, or education, one should still note that the goal of universal service in telephony is more consensual in the USA than in Britain (Hills, 1993, 186). This difference indicates that regulatory regimes sometimes allow the development and the promotion of social policies under regulatory regimes.

Paradoxically, study of the early regulatory regimes in Britain before the era of nationalization shows that Britain led the way in the design of industry-specific social regulations. British regulation has a long history, wrote Prosser, so long that it would be more accurate to see the period of nationalization as the exception amidst longer periods of regulatory controls (Prosser, 1997, 32). For example, the duty to connect people to the water networks was enforced in Britain as early as 1847 (Prosser, 1997, 40). The Electricity Act of 1882 required the laying of distribution mains for general supply on request (subject to certain conditions) and the supply of premises within 50 yards of such a main. It also limited disconnection from the electricity network to cases where there was not a *bona fide* dispute (Prosser, 1997, 149). Unfortunately, we lack comparative studies of the disconnection policies regarding unpaid bills in the United States and Britain for that period, yet there is no evidence that the private American corporations were quicker to disconnect then the state- owned distribution companies in Britain. Indeed, suggestions exist that centralization of policy and regulatory and service administrations into the hands of one central agency may create a friendly environment for management and labor but not for consumers. The clearer separation between private monopolies and the agency that which regulates them in the US may permit a louder voice for diffuse interests than the intimate network of a centralized ministry, which serves as both the policy maker, the regulator, and the service provider.

While common wisdom identifies nationalization with the rise of social-democratic and Marxist ideologies, this is only partly justified. While the entry of both the British and the American governments into the direct provision of electricity sometimes exerted important social effects - the rapid diffusion of electricity to rural areas - it is not the case in telecom. The gradual nationalization of the long-distance telephone network in 1896 and then the overall nationalization completed by 1911, were not aimed at social goals such as rapid diffusion and affordability. Back then the telephone was a luxury, a toy for the rich households and a tool for commercial businesses. When one could spend $20 to employ a maid for a year, or to pay the annual household expenses on electricity, coal, and wood, having unlimited telephone use for $17 did not seem a bargain (Perry, 1977, 78).[10] Why did the British government decide to nationalize telephony already in 1911, while it decided likewise for electricity only in 1947. While this is not the place to open the issue of reasons for nationalization, it is clear that nationalization was not motivated necessarily by the social welfare of the poor (cf. Millward, 1997).

The British and American regimes of ordered competition, especially in electricity, are too new for a summary of their social balance. The cry of "Delaware effect"[11] seems, however, exaggerated at least as regards the principles of regulation itself. Some signs of improvement in regulatory standards in electricity and telephony are telling in this regard. Telephone disconnections for debt by British Telecom stood at the amazing figure of 800,000, out of 20 million residential lines. Oftel's policy paper set the target for reduction of the number of disconnections at 50% per annum at least for the years 1998-1999 (Oftel, 1997). It also required British Telecom to offer to its customers a limited service of incoming calls only when a customer agreed on the repayment of her debt. Successes have already been recorded in electricity disconnections. Before privatization, disconnections were running at the rate of 70,000 a year. Disconnections since then have exhibited a certain steady and remarkable decline. In 1995-6 only 674 customers were disconnected for non-payment of bills. While some of the reduction was the result of a shift to prepayment electricity meters, most of it was due to policies of the electricity regulator (Prosser, 1997, 173). While the major beneficiaries of electricity liberalization are still the managers of the utilities and the big industrial and commercial consumers (MacKerron and Watson, 1996) there is reason to believe that these benefits can be extended to small consumers also. Problems of regulatory failure, such as the windfall profits of the utilities, can be fixed by special taxes, as was proved by the Labor Government (Doern and Wilks, 1998, 11-12).

The design of the regimes of ordered competition in telecom reveals clearly the potential of integrating social with economic regulations. The questions of Universal Service were part of the regime design in both the UK and the US. The integration of

---

[10] This situation in US was some what better but still telephone was a luxury. In 1896 telephone service in NY City cost $20 a month while average monthly income of a worker was $38.50 (Pool, I. Forecasting the Telephone: A Retrospective Technology Assessment, Alberx, 1983, p. 22. Schiller, 1998, 400-1).

[11] Or race to the bottom, that is, erosion on regulatory standards, see in relations to trade policies (Vogel, 1995). The same issue was examined in relation to British electricity environmental regulations by Collier. She found out that the electricity privatization was a mixed blessing in environmental terms. The lessons are that privatization and liberalization *per se* are not necessarily a problem but the is a definite need for a strong commitment to sound environmental regulations (Collier, 1995). In the US, under title XII of the 1992 Energy Act, the government will pay producers of electricity from certain renewable resources a "production incentive payment" or provide tax credits. This subsidy, coupled with technological improvement, is apt to rekindle the market for renewable electricity (Gilbert and Kahn, 1994, 205).

universal service provisions to the new telecom regime was aimed to ensure that increasing competition in the urban areas will not end up with increasing prices for the (geographic as well as social and economic) periphery. For this purposes the regulations in both the UK and the US moved to ensure the establishment of "equalization" Universal Services funds. The Americans went even further and are currently institutionalizing a regime for rate-subsidies of broadband services for schools, libraries and rural health care providers (for tele-medicine applications). True, the achievements in this sphere are less ambitious then what was hoped for by public interests groups, but this is the outcome of a right-wing dominated Congress rather than a problem of regulatory capacities (Drake, 1997). In addition, the increasing importance broadband services[12] - in the context of information society and information economy - means that in order to avoid widening gaps between info-rich and info-poor, special provisions to make these service affordable are necessary. In neither country do universal service provisions deal with this problem at the moment. Yet the potential for a more developed universal service regime is a possible outcome of more socially aware regulatory regimes, without necessary recourse to nationalization.

Thus, the common wisdom that places a higher social value on etatist provisions of regulatory services than on regulation is based on misleading generalization. This common wisdom reflects a concrete historical development in which welfare regimes were developed in Britain and Europe more rapidly and comprehensively than in the United States. The fact that at the same time that the Europeans created their welfare regimes they also nationalized extensively does not *necessarily* suggest that nationalization was motivated by social goals and definitely that these social goals could not be maximized by other methods of governance. The rise of current regulatory regimes as a solution for market failures should not be identified too closely with the particular (and exceptional) experience of the American State-formation. While the current regimes of ordered competition are still consolidating we have no definitive evidence that they supply socially inferior results (except for the employees) than those of the monopolistic regimes.

IV. The Rise of the Competition State

While both telecom and electricity have experienced considerable changes, it is electricity, far more than telecom, that demonstrates the strength of the forces shaping today's political order. This may sound surprising as electricity is moving slower towards competitive order.[13] Yet when one considers the technological incentives for competition in telecom, it becomes clear that the political will to transform electricity is the more

---

[12] For example, high speed internet for video, graphic and special applications.

[13] See Schmidt (1997) as to the European Union and OECD (1997) for a sectoral updates.

impressive.[14] In electricity, despite innovations such as the combined cycle gas turbine, which decreased the economics of scale, the incentives for competition were much more limited than in telecom. First, economically feasible alternatives to the copper wire of telephony are available to an extent that does not exist in electricity. Mobile telephony, satellite, and cable telephony provide alternative networks to wire and may serve as competitive systems. Second, technology offers new options for using electricity grids for the transmission of telecom data (packet-switching) and new options to electricity (and railway) companies to use their internal communication systems (and right-of-way) to supply telecom services. It is possible to use the electricity grids to transfer telecom but not the reverse. This implies that telecom companies may face competition from electricity companies that will use their grids and rights-of-way as strategic resources. Third, electricity transportation is sensitive to distance in a way that is unknown in telecom.[15] Transmission losses and the considerable costs involved in the construction of electricity transformers facilitate competitive pressures from distant generators. Fourth, the transportation of electricity requires grids that cost about ten times more than the transportation of telecom. This strengthens the sensitivity of electricity to distance and reduces the extent to which it can be traded economically (Levi-Faur, 1999b, 141-143).

The relatively weak technological and economic incentives for competition in electricity make the change in this sector so meaningful for political scientists. The autonomy of politics is paradoxically demonstrated better in this sphere, which is only slowly moving towards competition. It is in the sphere of utilities - water, gas, electricity, telecom, and railways - that countries converged on nationalization (Foreman-Peck and Millward, 1994, 8). Governments have grown bigger in this economic sphere more than in any other, so here the trends towards new governance regimes are the most telling. To the extent that the change identified in this paper is evident, what we see is a rise of new political order, namely the competition state (Levi-Faur, 1998). The competition state is an amalgamation of regimes of ordered competition in different spheres of economic and social activity and it is accommodated and embedded in the wider institutional setting of the nation-state. International governance structures that make competition laws and sector-specific regulation a matter for international agreements make the competition state a European and global rather than an Anglo-Saxon phenomenon (Akbar and Mueller, 1997; McGowan and Wilks, 1995; Nicolaides, 1997; Scherer, 1994).

While the term "competition state" may be used synonymously with "liberal state" (e.g., Cerny, 1990; 1997) this is not the meaning that it carries here. The competition state is highly interventionist and represents a new renaissance of the nation-state rather than its retreat. The history of the American telecom regime, particularly the period of dual service competition of 1894-1924, is indicative. The comparison between the role of the

[14] This does not mean that in telecom reform was pre-determined by technological change. Technological changes did not dictate or even create pressures for change in telecom. New technologies supplied no more than positive incentives for telecom liberalization that made regime change an attractive option.

[15] In the first days of telephony the technology was effective for a distance of only a few kilometers. In time, this sensitivity to distance became far less important. While new technologies reduce the sensitivity of electricity to distance across time, it is still far more sensitive than telecom (one critical problem is the rise in energy losses with distance).

state in that period and its role nowadays reveals the highly interventionist nature of the current political order. The expiry of Bell's patents in 1893 and 1894 was followed by the emergence of thousands of "independent" telephone companies. From 1900 to 1915 at least 45 percent of the US cities with populations over 5,000 had competing non-interconnected telephone exchanges. During the peak of this competitive period, between 1902 and 1910, the percentage was more than 55 (Mueller, 1997, 7). By 1907 the Bell system had less than 50% of the telephones in the United States (Bickers, 1991, 86). The competition took mainly the form of "dual service", namely the existence of two independent networks. Thus, subscribers who joined one system could not call subscribers of the other - unless, as happened about 13% of the time - they subscribed to both systems (Mueller, 1997, 7).

The obvious solution to the existence of two networks was the creation of interconnection agreements that would allow the subscriber of one network to interconnect with the subscriber of the other. However, the interests of the dominant Bell system in interconnection were hardly identical with those of new entrants to the telephone market. As the value of a telephone network grows in direct relation to the number of subscribers, the importance of interconnection for a small network to a bigger one is much greater than the reverse. In other words, AT&T had no incentive to connect its network to the networks of the independents, and usually did not do so even for areas where it did not offer services (Gabel, 1969, 341). The situation called for an interconnection regime in which a third party would enforce interconnection and determine its technical and economic terms. Some considerable efforts were made at the time in this direction, and while in 1910 only ten states had statutes regulating interconnection by 1919 this number had risen to 34 (Cohen, 1991, 60-61). Still, the form of interconnection at that time reveals the low policy capacities of the state commissions to create an effective regime. Interconnection legislation was under state rather than a federal jurisdiction, was challenged often at the courts as "confiscation of property", was very often restricted to the long-distance component (and not to local competing networks), and did not determine the technical and economic conditions of interconnecting the networks.

The differences from the interconnection regime that was devised by the 1996 Act and by FCC regulations tell much about the active role of the state in promoting telecom competition nowadays. The regulatory regime for interconnection is now a federal responsibility. This regime encompasses not only long-distance calls but also local exchanges. But perhaps the most important features in regard to the extent of state intervention are the requirements to unbundle the services at any "technically feasible point" and the mandate that the FCC has acquired as to the tariffs of interconnection. The requirement to unbundle means that competitors don't have to build their own network but can largely rely on each other's equipment. Digital exchange networks are highly expensive systems, which provide a wide variety of services such as advance signaling, diagnostic and testing procedures, switching, and transport. Telephone operators may ask to buy services from a competing operator (e.g., switching but not transporting, or signaling but not switching) and the legislation determines the duty to supply. More important, the FCC has the authority to set the benchmark prices of these different services. It thus has extended its regulatory role from retail to wholesale prices of telecom services. An equivalent regulation in the field of the car industry, just to give an example, would be the duty of Honda to sell any part of its engines to GM at prices determined fair by the Federal Trade Commission. Telecom regulation, therefore, goes here deeper and farther in determining what is technically feasible and economic desirable than ever before.

The interventionist nature of these so-called "deregulatory" reforms is not limited to telecommunications. Regulatory policies in electricity are now aimed at building a similar regime in electricity. Open access on demand for all to the transmission and distribution grids implies that the property rights of an operator are limited in the name of competition. Electricity suppliers will be able to compete with incumbents using their strategic assets. Moreover, as in the case of telecom the economic and technical conditions for interconnection will be under the discretion of regulatory agencies. This implies a different relation between regulation and competition from the one portrayed by George Stigler in the early 1970s. According to Stigler, "Regulation and competition are rhetorical friends and deadly enemies: over the doorway of every regulatory agency... should be carved: Competition Not Admitted".[16] This paper's account of the reforms in telecom and electricity presents a contrary picture. Regulation-for-competition is a necessary condition for the existence of competition in the telecom and the electricity sectors. It is not that Stigler's maxim doesn't capture the reality of the postwar regime; but it captures only it. Today's relations between regulation and competition are positive-sum, and over the doorway of every regulatory agency the term "Regulation-for-competition" should be carved. While much of the intellectual power for the regulatory reforms came from the Chicago economists, the result - regimes of ordered competition - is not necessarily what they had in mind.

The regimes of ordered competition are the product of various and sometimes conflicting political strategies such as privatization, regulation, deregulation, and reregulation. In contrast to the Chandler-Majone's thesis, the structures that represent the outcome of these strategies are not necessarily a direct outcome of the strategies. This is due to the fact that (a) these reforms involve policy learning and policy innovation, (b) unexpected obstacles and results are always part of the policy process, and (c) policy making and policy implementation are conducted over a relatively long period. The initiator of policy change is not necessary the one who carries it to its completion. But maybe the most important reason that liberalization is not identical with deregulation is the critical role of reregulation in these reforms. This is the component that gives so much power to the regulators and brings the state back in. Moreover, the sectoral regimes have to be accommodated to older state structures and institutions. This is why, despite the common characteristics of regimes of ordered competition, one may expect divergencies in the design of the regimes and in their outcome in terms of social and economic

[16] George J. Stigler "First Lecture", in Manuel F. Cohen and G. J. Stigler, *Can Regulatory Agencies Protect Consumers?* Washington, DC: American Enterprise Institute, 1971. Cited in MacAvoy W. Paul, The Failure of Antitrust and Regulation to Establish Competition in Long-Distance Services, The MIT Press and the AEI Press, 1996, p. xv

achievement. As with the study of divergencies in the welfare state, we will most probably have to study divergencies in the development of the competition state.

V. CONCLUSIONS: THE RISE OF THE COMPETITION STATE

Unlike Majone's conceptualization of change - from the positive to the regulatory state which examines the European developments in isolation from the American experience, this paper offers an alternative that captures both experiences and suggests the rise of the competition state as the best manifestation of the present-day change. Such a comprehensive framework of analysis is important, especially in view of the growing tendency to make the study of European politics a sub-discipline of the profession rather than an area study. The creation of regimes of ordered competition in telecom and electricity across countries and continents helps to put the EU regulatory developments in context, hence to distinguish its novel and exciting features from the more mundane.

The paper also points to the new structure of governance - that of ordered competition, which is not what economic liberals had in mind. Structures are not simply the results of strategies but also institutions that shape strategies. Outcomes are not only reflections of the balance of power between competing political agents with deliberate and premeditated strategies. They are also reflections of institutional, economic, and technological constraints, which are revealed only during the policy process. These regimes of ordered competition demonstrate the positive-sum relations between competition and regulation. In addition, they suggest a skeptical perspective towards predictions that the transformation from public ownership towards a regulated monopoly is leading the telecom and electricity regimes towards socially inferior results.

The study of the dynamics of American and British telecom and electricity regimes demonstrates the breadth of change in the architecture of the nation-state. The extent of change differs from sector to sector and country to country, yet often it is that difference that tells the most. While telecom has changed more than electricity and has become the symbol of the new information economy, it is the electricity reform, much less induced by technological incentives, that best exemplifies how comprehensive and politically-motivated these changes are. At the cross-national level, the British state has experienced the most striking changes. Privatization on the one hand and the creation of newly semi-independent regulatory agencies on the other represent a radical change from the past. Yet while Britain has experienced these most radical changes, the fact that the American telecom and electricity regimes have changed too, and that in electricity it is Britain that has led the way in the creation of regime of "ordered competition", is instructive. It demonstrates that the change is not simply a convergence on the American model and/or an outcome of the excessive power of American business community but also an open-ended process, which significantly involves policy learning.

While both states have changed their regimes their starting points were different. Britain started with restrictive regulatory regimes at the municipal level, and then moved towards etatism and direct provision of services by the state. America started with laissez-faire polices and then moved to the consolidation of regulatory regimes with private monopolies, first at the state level and then on the federal level. The terms that may best capture the variations in the trajectories of the American and British states in their dealing with telecom and electricity at the starting point of the first half of the 20th century is the regulatory state in America and the service-provision state in Britain. Other terms, like the interventionist state, the positive state, or even the administrative state, do not capture the different trajectories of the two countries and/or obstruct our understudying of the new architecture of the nation-state that has developed since the 1980s.[17] The new regimes of ordered competition in both the US and Britain are characterized best as the rise of the Competition State. To describe the changes in Britain as the rise of the regulatory state would be instructive to the extent that new regulatory structures are established, but it would be misleading as British regulatory expansion begun some centuries earlier, well before the 1980s. Hence, while the British trajectory may be described as movement from the Service-provision State to the Competition State, the American trajectory may be described as a movement from the Regulatory State to the Competition State.

The term Competition State does not connote metamorphosis of the state. It is best to talk in this sense about a change that adds a new institutional layer to a very thick structure that has taken shape over centuries. Like coral reefs, state structures are built and rebuilt down generations and are subject to forces of erosion and renewal at the same time. New layers are not simply overlaid but are accommodated. This is one reason why new divergencies are expected to occur and why structures do not simply follow strategies. Facing different state structures, the same strategies may result in different outcomes. Variances in structures and regime design against the background of different economic, social, and political environments will most probably affect the outcomes of the reforms. Thus, while the nation-state is forcing globalization back through the institutionalization of the Competition State, it does so, as before, in a way that ensures the perpetual generation of convergence and divergencies.

Interventionism and positivism have differed between the countries, and somewhat less between the sectors, but they were important across the countries and across the sectors. This is why Seidman and Gilmour (1986) on the one hand and Majone (1997) on the other characterized the postwar order in the US and Britain as positive and interventionist. But for political economists, probably in contrast to public administration specialists, direct or indirect provision of services could not represent the major feature of change. More significant are on the one hand the changes in the politics of ownership, centralization of power, and legitimization of monopolies, and on the other continuity of interventionism and positivism. The form of interventionism has changed, not its extent or even scope. Compared with the past, positivism is still an important characteristic of the current regimes of telecom and electricity. This is reflected in the potential for the promotion of life-line policies, the emphasis on universal service, and the continuity in

[17] Cerny's conceptualization of the transformation from Welfare State to Competition State (Cerny, 1990, 220) is not satisfying for our purpose either, because telecom and electricity etatism is not a major feature of the welfare state.

tariff-regulation. While the employees of British and American telecom and electricity paid a heavy price (layoffs, and decrease in job security for those who stayed) the consumers seem to be winning in telecom or may win in electricity.

DESIGNING ECONOMIC REGULATORY INSTITUTIONS FOR EUROPEAN NETWORK INDUSTRIES

David Coen and Chris Doyle
London Business School*

1. INTRODUCTION

Liberalisation of European network industries and the creation of a single market have witnessed European Union (EU) institutions taking on increased economic regulatory competencies (Doyle 1996, Majone 1996, McGowan and Wallace 1996). At the same time national regulatory authorities (NRAs) have been established in many industries, and competition legislation in Member States has evolved to shadow more closely the rules on competition in the European Treaty. All these changes have inevitably generated a more complex setting in which there are multiple tiers of regulation and business lobbying (Coen 1998, Heritier 1996, Richardson 1996). Under the principle of subsidiarity Member States are granted wide discretion in implementing European liberalisation and, arguably this has served to amplify complexity across the European Union.

The economic regulatory regime governing European network industries is further complicated by overlapping jurisdictions, notably the European Commission, the European Court of Justice (ECJ), the European Parliament, and Member State governments and their respective agencies. Many commentators are now questioning the efficacy of the current regulatory institutional framework and asking whether reforms could promote greater efficiency by encouraging more uniformity, simplicity and co-ordination (Majone 1996, Synder 1993).

In this paper we examine the design of the regulatory framework governing European network industries, taking account of structures that are more and less centralised than the status quo. We develop a framework within which the key criteria shaping regulatory structures are discussed. Given these criteria we are interested in addressing who is managing and who should be managing 'multi-level' regulation in Europe. Having outlined the criteria that ought to be satisfied by a 'good' regulatory regime, we argue

---

* This article was prepared for ECSA Pittsburgh 1999 panel Regulation in the EU and the LBS/MPI Anglo-German workshop on Economic Regulation and has benefitted from numerous comments from colleagues such as Nino Majone, Mark Thatcher and Martin Siner. The research was funded by the LBS Regulation Initative and the Anglo-German Foundation.

qualitatively that the institutional framework of regulation falls into one of four categories. We then assess how each of these categories performs in terms of the criteria we establish. Throughout our discussion the principle actors in the regulatory game are examined.

To facilitate this typology we draw on examples from some specific industries within the network industries sector, such as telecommunications, electricity and postal services. The size and importance of these industries is widely recognized and it is not surprising that politicians see them as playing a significant role in influencing key European objectives: sustaining economic growth, improving competitiveness and forging greater cohesiveness. These objectives have resulted in a multitude of policies reforming many aspects of European network industries.

The factors precipitating the change in policy towards the network industries have, to a large extent, been technologically and market driven. In many cases newer technology is enabling several firms to supply outputs efficiently. Natural monopoly, where a single firm is in a position to supply market demand at lowest production cost (i.e. efficiently), no longer pervades in many parts of the network industries. It is no longer inefficient in most power markets to have several firms generating electricity. Increasing demand for some services, notably in telecommunications, has also helped facilitate multi-firm supply and competition.

Inefficiency in some of Europe's network industries coupled with market structure changes has accommodated political acceptance of pro-competition measures. In some countries it would appear that politicians have largely paid lip service to liberalization. For the European economy as a whole to benefit from liberalisation it has been necessary to have a strong central body committed to initiating and co-ordinating pro-market reforms. Since the Single European Act of 1987 the European Commission (the 'Commission') has been committed to implementing liberalisation in Europe's network industries. Indeed, without the European Commission's efforts it is extremely doubtful whether Europe's economy would have benefited as much from changes affecting the network industries.

The Commission has been at the heart of the reform programme introducing competition. It has been able to strengthen its position as the initiator of reforms because it operates an increasingly sympathetic political climate. Political legitimacy resulted in the 1987 Single Act facilitating the first major initiatives. The Single Act mandated the Commission to devise policies bringing about a single market in communications, transport and energy. This required a legislative programme focused on liberalisation and harmonisation.[1] The programme of reforms was strengthened following the Treaty of European Union in 1992. The Commission accelerated its programme of liberalisation and harmonisation in the network industries in the middle 1990s. By 1998 almost all the necessary liberalization measures had been adopted and attention has shifted more towards implementation.

---

[1] Liberalisation establishes the conditions, or market rules, necessary for the operation of an internal or single market, and harmonisation is aimed at bringing consistency across what had hitherto been industries predominantly shaped by national markets.

Although the changing political landscape has unquestionably favoured reforms, another crucial factor helping to foster a competitive regime has been the changing corporate climate. Whereas at one time managers in most European network firms operated exclusively within their national territories, today many companies are keen to expand operations outside their traditional service areas. Managers in newly privatised companies in particular are keen to move into new markets. Even managers in publicly owned companies in network industries are engaging in ambitious expansion programmes. For example, Electricité de France has acquired private electricity companies in the United Kingdom.

In this article we are interested in who should and how can EU regulation of network industries be managed. In part 2 we discuss how the liberalisation in the single market has altered the nature of regulation and how equity and efficiency factors impact on regulation of Electricity, Gas, Postal Services and Telecommunications. Having recognised the need for regulation, part 3 proposes four alternative regulatory regimes - Current Regulatory Model, Federal Regulatory Commission, Regulatory Agency, and Regulatory Forums - and assesses how each interacts with the European and member state institutions. Finally, part 4 proposes a set of principles that should govern credible and effective regulation and constructs a simple qualitative cost benefit of the four competing regulatory regimes. We conclude by assessing the political and practical constraints of implementing a credible EU regulatory regime.

2. Efficiency, Equity and the Evolution of Regulation

Economic regulation is usually required (demanded) because 'free' markets fail to deliver desirable outcomes. Monopoly abuse in retail and wholesale markets may call for the level of prices to be regulated and discrimination across customers may lead to calls for regulation to affect the structure of prices. In the former case regulation is undertaken to achieve efficiency and in the latter case regulation is motivated by fairness or equity considerations. In Table 1 we highlight how efficiency and equity factors impact on regulation in four network industries.

As has been described elsewhere (see MED1 1998), liberalisation in Europe is resulting in network industries evolving along a path from monopoly (phase 1), to monopoly and competition (phase 2), and possibly to competition (phase 3). These three phases of market structure are described in Box 1, along with the industries and sectors associated with each phase.[2] It can be seen that there is considerable diversity across the industries. Air transport and telecommunications are highly liberalized, but most sectors within these industries have yet to progress into phase 3. Gas has not yet been liberalized, but in the near future it will enter phase 2. Most industries or sectors within industries currently lie in either phase 1 or phase 2 and this is likely to continue for some years to come.

---

[2] Box 1 characterises the formal position at a European level. In some Member States competition is much more extensive than that suggested by Box 1.

Table 1: Efficiency and equity grounds for regulation

Industry Characteristics	Equity Arguments	Efficiency Arguments
Electricity Non-storable. Some economies of scale. Demand slowly rising. Innovations in service provision, less in network.	Security of supply Universal service Geographic uniformity	Natural monopoly in transportation: transmission and distribution. Third party access to customers. Incumbency dominance.
Gas Storable. Demand rising as an input to electric generation. Innovations minimal.	Security of supply Universal service Geographic uniformity	Natural monopoly in transportation. Third party access to customers. Incumbency dominance.
Postal Services Demand rising, innovations affecting sorting and tracking processes.	Universal service Geographic uniformity	Natural monopoly local delivery network. Incumbency dominance.
Telecommunications Demand growing significantly, due especially to internet. Innovations significantly affecting industry. Convergence across fixed and mobile, and horizontally with IT and media sectors.	Universal service Geographic uniformity Access to information society	Natural monopoly in some elements of the local loop (depends on demand and population density) and scarce resources (eg. radio spectrum). Incumbency dominance.

Phase 1 – Monopoly: One firm supplies services.
Airports, ports, most rail services and rail infrastructure, gas, reserved postal services and water.

Phase 2 – Monopoly & Competition: Competition is gradually introduced into some or all markets.
Airport ground handling facilities, electricity, port-handling facilities, some rail freight markets, most air services, and residential telecommunications.

Phase 3 – Competition: Here competition is extensive and increasingly effective and sustainable in some or all markets.
Some air and shipping services, business telecommunications services, and non-reserved postal services.

Box 1: The evolution of competition

The introduction of competition in network industries necessitates a corresponding increase in regulatory activity in the short term because of the presence of powerful incumbent firms. Over time it is expected that competition will become more effective and the scale and scope of regulatory activity correspondingly decline. In Box 2 we describe the evolution of regulatory activity over the three phases of market structure.

Phase 1 – Monopoly: Regulation is concerned with the prevention of monopoly abuse in retail markets and the attainment of public service objectives (e.g. universal service).

Phase 2 – Monopoly & Competition: Regulation focuses on: monopolies abuse in both retail and interconnect markets by dominant incumbents; emerging competition issues; and public service obligations.

Phase 3 – Competition: Some light-handed regulation is needed, as in other competitive markets, to ensure fair trading practices and the maintenance of public service objectives.

Box 2: The evolution of regulatory activity

A number of articles in the EC Treaty (last updated in May 1999 following the implementation of the Amsterdam Treaty) are applicable to network industries. Over time some articles have become more relevant following liberalization, in particular the articles outlining the rules on competition, especially Articles 81 and 82. These are summarised in Box 3.

- *General Economic Interest:* Article 16 (fulfil their missions).
- *Rules on Competition:* Articles 81 (restrictive practices), 82 (dominance) and 86 (exclusive rights).
- *Aids granted by States:* Articles 87-89.
- *Approximation of Laws:* Article 95 (internal market).
- *Trans European Networks:* Articles 154 (interconnection and interoperability), 155 (guidelines and standards) and 156 (consultation procedures).
- *Industry:* Article 157 (competitiveness and adjustment).

Box 3: EC Treaty Articles relevant to network industries

In Table 2 we outline the main European legislative measures that have been taken in some of the key network industries.

Table 2: European Legislation in the Network Industries

Industry	Liberalization and Competition Measures	Current Status of Competition in Europe
Electricity	Some measures in the early 1990s. Directive 96/62/EC gradually opening up the market. White Paper on renewable sources of energy, November 1997. Market liberalisation started February 1999.	Gradual liberalization benefiting large users began February 1999. Industry in phase 2, although in some Member States liberalisation has proceeded much further than EU timetable.
Natural Gas	Directive 98/30/EC along the same lines as electricity.	Gradual approach to liberalization. Industry will enter phase 2 from 10 August 2000. Some Member States like the UK already in phase 2 and approaching phase 3.
Postal Services	Directive 97/67/EC and Notice on the application of competition rules. Further liberalization to occur by 2003.	Segmented market: very competitive high value (non-reserved) sector mainly in phase 3; reserved sector in phase 1.
Telecommun-ications	Many liberalization and harmonization measures between 1987 and 1998. Review in 1999.	Services and infrastructure fully liberalized and market in phase 2, many parts moving towards or in phase 3. (Excluding Greece and Portugal.)

The detailed legislation that has been passed at the European level has been accompanied by considerable national legislation. These measures and the complexity of network industries justify sector specific regulation. The main issue facing policy makers is the nature such regulation should take.

3. CREDIBLE REGULATORY INSTITUTIONS IN THE MULTI-LEVEL EU

If the newly liberalised network industries are to operate efficiently and equitably it is important that EU and member states have effective institutional structures and procedures in place.

Led by the Council of Ministers, the European Commission and increasingly the European Parliament, it has become very apparent that similar economic frameworks, legal principles and political goals are relevant across the single market (Pelkman 1997 and Hancher 1996). What is less apparent are the forms such regulatory institutions should take and what structures are feasible. Should regulatory institutions be increasingly integrated and operated at a central level through some formal European body? Alternatively, should regulation be largely devolved to national regulatory bodies? If a European body were acceptable, should it operate as a stand-alone institution or a pan-European organisation - that is the sum of national regulatory bodies?

The choices available regarding regulatory development in the EU naturally generate ambiguity. Sir Iain Vallance, Chairman of BT, captures this in a recent quotation:

> *"... the Commission, and specifically DGIV, must have the power to ensure the single market is completed while rooting out state aids. It has been suggested that the creation of a European Cartel office might offer a partial solution. I personally do not believe the case for this has yet been proven. Nothing in BT's dealings with the Commission has offered unequivocal proof that it cannot handle big competition cases without undue political interference. That said, a pan European agency for telecommunications sector could perhaps be desirable in the longer term as the Single Market strengthens. The alternative of 15 regulators taking 15 different approaches to the promotion of consumer interests and competition does not sit altogether comfortably with the single market ideal. Consistency is essential for a genuine Single Market, but a good and politically realistic halfway house might be a committee of national regulators, perhaps chaired by a Commissioner, exchanging best regulatory practices and ideas and assessing cross-border issues."* Phillip Morris speech (1996)

Accepting that there is variance across countries, size of firms, and nature of markets, we construct a qualitative cost-benefit analysis for a variety of potential EU regulatory regimes. Recognising that regulation must take into consideration trade-offs between equity and efficiency, deter unfair competition, and minimise undue political intervention, we propose a number of regulatory characteristics that facilitate credible and effective regulation and assess their practical implementation for four potential EU regulatory regimes:

- Current Regulatory Regime - European principles, national implementation and shared responsibilities for enforcement.
- Federal Regulatory Commission - European principles, European implementation and European enforcement.
- Regulatory Agency - European principles, European led implementation and enforcement.
- Regulatory Forum - European principles, National led implementation and enforcement.

3.1 Current Regulatory Regime

At present the EU regulatory regime consists of a number of national regulatory bodies that interact with business, consumers, national governments and European institutions. Under these conditions it is possible to see a hierarchical pattern appearing as illustrated in Figure 1. In this multilevel model, firms make representation to the national regulatory authorities - which deal with pricing and consumer issues; national government - which determines the normative goals of regulation; and EU institutions - which focus on regulating the member states via judgements on competition policy and levels of state aid.

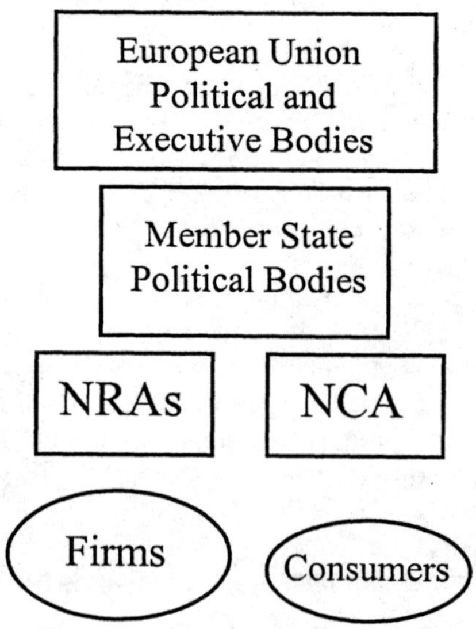

Figure 1: Current Regulatory Regime

Significantly, while the Commission has encouraged liberalisation and exerted pressure on macroeconomic convergence criteria, they have not sought to harmonise formal regulatory institutions. Instead the Commission has recognised that while large disparities in institutional powers, procedures and resources exist between NRAs across sector and country - as illustrated in Table 3 - they are important in framing and implementing regulation in the national markets.[3] However, these national differences have large implications for the speed of liberalisation in each member state and the degree of competition (Bergman et al 1998 and Pelkman 1997).

Table 3: National Regulatory Regimes

	Energy	Telecom	PTT	Rail
France	Direction générale de' lectricity Matieres Premere In February 2000, Parliament passes a statute to introduce a single regulatory agency.	Autorite de Regulation des Telecommunication (ART) & Ministry	Ministry of Economy, Finance and Industry.	Ministry of Equipment, Transport and Tourism
Germany	Federal Cartel Office (Budeskartellamt), German Ministry of Commerce and Länder	Regulierungsbehörde für Telekommunikation und Post.	Regulierungsbe hörde für Telekommunika tion und Post Ministry and Länder	Eisenbahn Bundesant, German Ministry of Transport and Länder
UK	OFGEM, Office of gas and electricity markets	OFTEL Office of Telecommunications & DTI	DTI. Department of trade & industry. A draft bill on postal services recommended a regulator	ORR Office of Rail regulator & SRA Strategic Regulatory Authority.

While Germany has thus far preferred to regulate the majority of its sectors via its cartel and commerce ministries, the UK has chosen to establish independent regulatory agencies and France, interestingly, has taken a more mix and match approach to regulation as demonstrated by the developments in the energy sector.[4] While, European economic convergence pressures can be observed, in the spirit of subsidiarity the

[3] See the COM (1999) 537 11 November 1999 Fifth Report on the Implementation of the Telecommunications Regulatory Package.

[4] For a description of regulatory models in Germany see Eberlin in this issue and for a discussion of the independent regulatory agencies in the UK see Thatcher 1997 and 1998.

Commission recognises that NRA's have numerous responsibilities and an expertise of national markets. For example mutual recognition exists in the drafting and granting authorisation to enter a national market; dealing and offering procedures to deal with disputes between operators or between an operator and its customers. Consequently, the existing EU regulatory system provides a large degree of discretion while attempting to ensure that services are affordable and equitable.

Where there has been convergence, as in Telecoms, it would appear that it was more a function of the economic structural aspects of directives than an explicit request for institutional uniformity. For example, while Article 7 states that: "*Member states shall ensure that from the 1 July 1991 the granting of operating licences, the control of type approval and mandatory specifications, the allocation of frequencies and surveillance of usage conditions are carried out by a body independent of the telecommunications organisations.*"[5] Agencies' actual powers and independence from national government vary dramatically.

Clearly, the Commission has chosen to focus on the business issues of market access and structure and has attempted to work with, rather than harmonise, the member states' regulatory regimes. In a recent speech Jean Francois Pons the deputy director of Competition at the European Commission observed: "*The Commission's notice on the application of competition rules to access agreements in the telecommunications sector" (The Access Notices) deals with the relationship between the application of competition rules and sector-specific regulation as well as procedural issues regarding access agreements in the telecommunications sector. It notably set out (para 28) that the priority should be given to sector-specific regulation applied by NRAs where applicable and subject to the rights of companies to complain under the competition rules*".

Significantly, the Commission will not initiate any investigation into infringements of EU competition rules, but rather monitors cases and allows the NRAs to remedy issues. This is consistent with the Commission's belief that EU Competition law incorporates strong elements of subsidiarity. As Sir Leon Brittan observed "*subsidiarity has always been the central pillar upon which the Jurisdictional divide between the Community and the member states in the field of competition policy is based.*"[6] However, the Commission will intervene if the NRAs take an unreasonable amount of time (approximately 6 months), or if the case has a substantial Community interest - i.e. affects competition in a number of member states. The Commission therefore monitors NRAs' judgements to check they are consistent with pricing practices in articles 81 and article 82. As a result of the above, the existing multinational/institutional regulatory procedures score badly in terms of speed and procedural clarity and place undue pressures on new entrants.

It is these new entrants who created the greatest pressure for institutional regulatory reform in Europe. Initially, new entrants promoted the primacy of European competition law as a means of accessing markets - but in the process they created the 'first supranational policy' regime of the EU (McGowan and Wilks 1996). Secondly, as Levi-Faur noted the telecommunication industry has promoted "*A draft of a directive which*

---

[5] ONP Directive 90/388/EC

[6] Laudati 1996 p247 quotes from the Antitrust &Trade Regulation Rep. (BNA), N0.63 at 150 of 30th.

aims at creating a self-certification regime, as well as a single "one-stop" conformity assessment procedure, has already been prepared by the Commission. If approved, this new regime will transform the relations between the European manufactures and the Community." (Levi-Faur 1999:113). This directive would place the issues of safety, health and interoperability of telecommunication equipment under EU consumer protection legislation and would give business a great deal of lobbying flexibility in playing the regulatory game.

By setting only broad duties and objectives, European objectives will give a large degree of flexibility to member states and business interests (who move at different regulatory speeds) and allow for regulatory diversity within Europe. However, while it avoids the problems of the role of national competition law and different ministries/agencies, it creates a level playing field through consistent monitoring and the European courts. The existing EU model has the advantage of allowing national cultural variance to continue and has a medium to high level of political legitimacy, but it suffers from the increasing risk of multiple-level business lobbying, problems of transparency and accountability, and the risk of 'regulatory competition' between national regulatory bodies. Moreover, its over reliance on courts reduces flexibility and the possibility of self-regulation and co-operation.

3.2 Federal Regulatory Commission

A possible reform of the existing European regulatory regime would be the introduction of a federal regulatory system. This would give clear powers to the FRC to co-ordinate and legislate on matters of EU economic regulation. As figure 2 suggests, it would operate as an umbrella organisation over similar NRAs and NCAs. This has the benefit of greater clarity of procedure and accountability within the regulatory regime, but it does make the regulatory process more rigid. Moreover, there is a risk that a federal system, that is merely the sum of the NRAs, would suffer in terms of speed and flexibility as a result of 'lowest common denominator' compromises between NRAs and member states. Yet, conversely such a regulatory regime has a high level of legitimacy and credibility if the sole criteria are economic efficiency and represents a fully integrated policy process.

Some member states, such as Germany and Italy, have suggested that DG IV could gradually evolve into a European Competition Authority independent of national and European bodies (Majone 1997). This would avoid the potential political games that have occurred at the Commission and create a clear regulatory hierarchy. The model most often cited is the German cartel office with its constitutional political independence and procedural transparency.[7] However, for this new institution to be created and work effectively, we would require significant changes to European treaties. Yet, once created,

[7] See Everson 1996 p210-215. As Majone notes while the German Federal Cartel Office itself is not immune from political influence, the procedures that a government must follow are so transparent that to change a judgement incurs high political costs.

a federal cartel office would still suffer from limited political legitimacy in member states and enforcement of its judgements would vary - depending upon traditions of competition law (Ehlermann 1995).

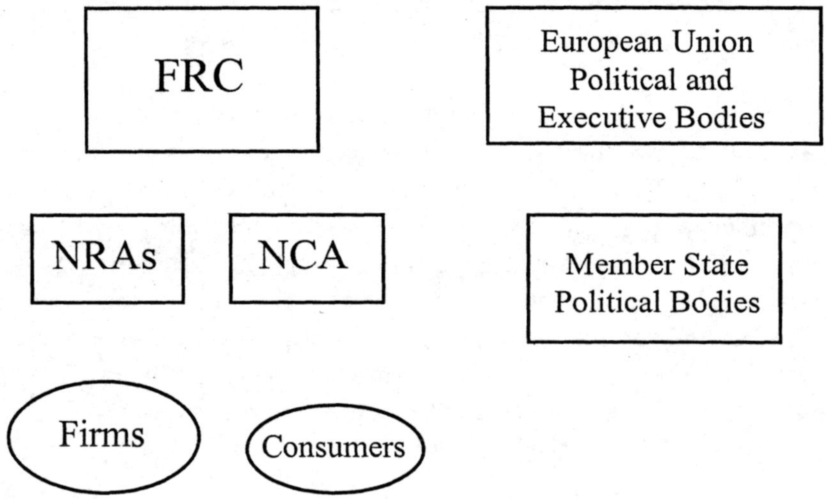

Figure 2: Federal Regulatory Commission

In terms of practical application, it is significant that each of the utility sectors would require individual regulatory organisations and that much of the costs of EU regulation in terms of implementation and compliance could still be passed on to NRAs. However, it is reasonable to assume that member states with no tradition of agency would be reluctant to concede power to such an autonomous body. The Commission may also show reluctance to delegate regulatory competencies to another independent regulatory body without some oversight or judicial review.

3.3 Regulatory Agency

A possible solution to the risk of national compromises in the regulatory market is to establish a European Regulatory Agency with independence from European Institutions and member states. Such a body could incorporate existing national regulatory bodies to allow for some national variance. Assuming that the European regulatory agency was given judicial powers and autonomy, it would benefit from not waiting for NRAs to enforce common directives. In this uniformed environment it is possible to envisage higher levels of trust between member states (Everson 1995, 1997 and Majone 1996). But, within the context of the democratic deficit in Europe a number of important questions must be raised about responsibility and accountability (Egan 1998, Majone 1997, Everson 1997, Shapiro 1997).

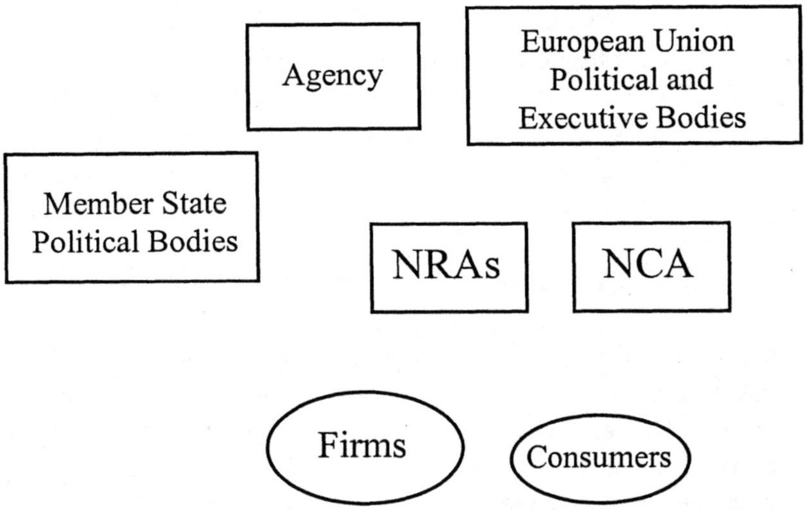

Figure 3: European Regulatory Agency

In recent years, we have seen the introduction of ten such bodies, for example the European Environment Agency, the European Agency for the evaluation of medicinal products and the European vocational training foundation (Kreher 1996). The agency solution can be justified in efficiency terms if we accept the hypothesis that agents have substantive knowledge and informational advantages (Mitnick 1993). In a policy area like economic regulation where we have a high degree of technical expertise and knowledge, the creation of a specialised body can have large economies of information. Moreover, the creation of an independent agency will allow governments, who are under increasing EU macro convergence pressure, to pass on the responsibility for difficult political decisions regarding subsidies and markets access. Therefore, European agencies by co-ordinating the European regulatory environment can help to minimises the potential regulatory "races to the bottom" and subsequent market failures between member states. Recognising some of the potential benefits the European Parliament has requested that the European Commission look into the possibility for independent regulatory bodies in the utility sectors.[8] The European Commission, while reluctant to hand over executive

[8] For example, the EP inserted this requirement into article 22 of Directive 97/33/EC of June 1997 on Interconnection in Telecommunications with regard to universal services and interoperability through application of the principles of Open Network Provision (ONP) (OJ199/32 26.07.97). They also introduced into article 8 of the Council Directive 90/387/EEC on the establishment of Open Network Provision (90/387/EEC, OJ L192/1, 24.07.9o, as amended by Directive 97/51/EC. OJ L 295/23. 29.10.97.

powers to a new regulatory body has commissioned a number of studies of actors' preferences and favours the maintaining the regulatory status quo.[9]

However, there are a number of problems in creating an agency. In addition to the diversity in government business relations in member states and lack of a European tradition in the use of statutory competition law, we are faced with political difficulties in altering European Treaties for new institutional bodies (Everson 1995 and Majone 1996). What is more, as previously noted, the EU has traditionally taken a decentralised and legislative approach to integration and has relied on implementation by member states (Majone 1996, Dehousse et al 1992). It is therefore unlikely that national governments would quietly accept the introduction of independent rule-making agencies at the present time.

With the creation of current regulatory agencies, the Commission has circumvented some of these problems by delegating executive functions to the agencies, while maintaining oversight and final judicial control. In terms of legitimacy, agencies can be viewed as yet another unelected European institution or as an independent institution of appropriate size and positioning to regulate the single market - only time and court cases will tell. Unquestionably an agency improves the accountability, transparency and clarity of EU regulation as they remove the different levels of enforcement.

3.4 Regulatory Forums: Informal Networks of Regulation

With the reluctance of many national governments to hand over full regulatory control, co-operation between national regulatory bodies offers a temporary solution and may illustrate the long run benefits of formal co-ordination at the European level. While, at the present time, the Commission recognises that many of the regulatory problems must be tackled at both the national and European level, it also recognises that it is possible to encourage the emergence of transitional regulatory networks. Majone argues that while individual NRAs are weak and susceptible to domestic political pressure, if they are integrated into a European network of regulators, they gain collective strength. *"This is because the regulators have an incentive to maintain their reputation in the eyes of fellow regulators in other countries; a politically motivated decision would compromise their credibility and render co-operation more difficult to achieve in the future." Majone 1996:273* These networks could be informally co-ordinated by voluntary regulatory forums that gradually encourage the standardisation of NRAs and facilitate the establishment of European regulatory norms by defining operating frameworks.

---

[9] For example the recent report prepared by Eurostrategies for the European Commission on "the possible added value of European Regulatory Authority for Telecommunications. September 1999.

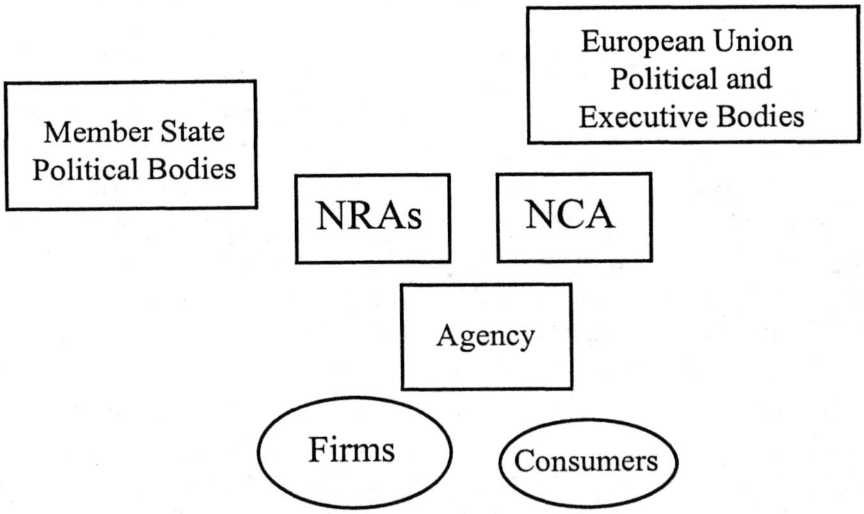

Figure 4: Regulatory Forum

At present, the Commission has created a number of committees of standing experts. In the case of Telecommunications, DGIV and DGXIII have been active in establishing groups like the ONP Committee. Meeting once every 2 months, and made up of member state governments ministries, permanent representatives, NRAs and Commission officials, the ONP Committee is primarily involved in monitoring issues of licensing and implementation but is gradually taking on more substantial regulatory roles. Based on the success of existing committees and the commissioned studies on the value added of a EU regulator, the European Commission proposed in November 1999 to improve existing co-operation between the Commission and NRAs.[10] The 1999 Communications review proposed that "*Increased delegation of decisions-making to NRAs requires a counterbalance in the form of greater co-ordination of the NRA decisions and positions at the EU level. Such co-ordination should in the first instance rely on consensus building process among European regulators in which all interested parties are able to state their views. Ultimately, however, such consensus building will only be truly effective if it is backed up by the possibility to give decisions legal force" (COM 1999.539 p51).* To facilitate this new consensus building the Commission has proposed to establish two new regulatory committees. The two-part structural development comprises of a formal committee, made up of Commission and member states, the communication committee

[10] See, "Towards a new framework for Electronic Communications infrastructure and associated services" The 1999 Communications Review Com. (1999) 539.

(COCOM), and a High level Communication Group (HLCG) composed of NRAs and the Commission.[11]

It is envisaged that COCOM would replace the existing ONP and licensing committee and would have advisory powers. In this advisory capacity COCOM would present opinions to the Commission on draft measures of a non-binding nature and HLCG and other expert groups would provide comments. In its regulatory capacity, COCOM would vote on draft measures of a binding nature after receiving requests from HLCG. The HLCG is a formal replacement for the current ad-hoc High Level Regulators Group and would be the sum of the NRAs with the Commission acting as a secretariat. Its aim would be to build consensus among divergent NRAs and to mediate with economic and social interests like the ERT and European Consumer groups, and liase with EU institutions like the EP and Council. It is hoped that this consensus building approach will harmonise implementation and EU regulatory codes of practice.

However, while these forums provide the opportunity for co-ordinated EU regulation many of the issues are no longer confined to the single market. As David Edmonds the Director General of OFTEL notes: "*We need strong co-operation between NRAs to deal with international issues....I think (International Regulatory Group) IRG has got off to a good start. But we need to find ways of convincing interested parties that the NRAs can and will co-operate so that similar problems get dealt with similarly in all parts of the Community. Otherwise there is bound to be pressure for a Euro-regulator- even though this would be a second-best solution.*"

It is hoped that these committees and co-ordination networks will gradually encourage procedural convergence and harmonisation of regulatory experts' goals. The networks will improve information and personnel flows between countries and create a more stable regulatory environment. Such regulatory developments have the advantage of being incrementally accepted by member states, EU institutions and the public. Moreover, by avoiding hard political choices and conflicts the networks allow for the development of trust and understanding. While representing the status quo, the incremental forum networks may gradually evolve into more formalised independent European regulatory bodies.

Nevertheless, the opaque and at times arbitrary membership of some of the existing EU committees raises a number of questions marks about their accountability and transparency and over time may undermine their legitimacy and ability to enforce judgements. Consequently, while we can expect quicker decision-making and implementation, the low jurisdictional transparency will result in calls - from industry and member states - for increasingly formal regulatory arrangements like COCOM and HLCG.

---

[11] These committees would work under the new comitology arrangements agreed by the EP, Council and Commission in June 1999. (OJ L 184, 17.07.99 "The Comitogy Decision")

4. A Qualitative Cost-Benefit Analysis of the Regulatory Regimes

The criteria we propose for a credible regulatory regime are as follows:

- Independence. This refers to the regulator's protection from undue direct political interference in its operations. In the case of an EU regulatory regime it is important to assess the degree to which national regulatory bodies are free from direct political interference in each member state and the degree to which a European regulatory body would be insulated from national pressures pushing-up and European institutional pressures from the Commission and Parliament.
- Enforcement Powers. At present the European Commission requires through Article 226 of the Treaty that member states implement directives and has the power under section 228 of the Treaty to fine those states that fail (Synder 1993, Weiler 1992). However, the complexity and lack of speed of legal processes at a European level undermines the credible sanctioning of states and firms. The discussion of the balance of enforcement between the Commission and Member states therefore requires greater clarity, whatever the regulatory regime in place, to ensure that companies face credible deterrents and member states do not attempt to gain regulatory advantage.
- Legitimacy. A regulatory regime must avoid ambiguity. It must therefore have clear appeal mechanisms, clear review processes, and consistent judgements. Legitimacy is best achieved through long run commitment to impartial regulation. Any EU regulatory body must recognise that its democratic mandate is limited in comparison with that of an elected member state parliament - or even the European parliament.
- Accountability. To maintain independence and credibility it is important that the regulatory bodies are subject to judicial review. However, the advantages of the various national and European courts, national governments and European institutions must be assessed. Accountability of any new EU regulatory body would face the additional problem of democratic deficit.
- Transparency. Credibility is greatly enhanced in a clear and open system where the process is understood and respected. Transparency facilitates the development of trust and the flow of information. Moreover, it may alleviate some of the accountability problems and reduce the risk of regulatory capture by business.
- Clear and well-defined objectives. This will enable the public and regulated companies to understand the regulatory regime. In avoiding ambiguity, firms will understand better the rules of engagement and policy making should operate more speedily. Clear and well-defined objectives should establish trust for all parties in the system. EU regulation has thus far suffered due to the number of levels and institutions involved in the regulatory process. Moreover, the

bureaucratic and often opaque nature of the Commission limits the appeal as a single supranational regulatory body.[12]

The above criteria constitute a set of principles that should govern a credible regulatory regime. Using these principles we examine the four regulatory regimes according to whether they exhibit high (3 points), medium (2 points) or low (1 point) tendencies towards the characteristics identified. We attribute a simple credibility rating for each of the options and calculate a credibility rating.

Table 3: Credible European Regulation

Characteristics	Current Regulatory Regime	Federal Regulatory Commission	Regulatory Agency	Regulatory Forum
Independence	Low-Medium	High	Low-Medium	Low-medium
Enforcement	Medium	Medium	Low-Medium	Medium-high
Legitimacy	Medium-High	High	Medium-High	Medium
Accountability	Low-Medium	Medium	Medium-High	Low
Transparency	Medium	Low	Medium	Low
Clarity	Medium	Medium	Medium	Low-medium
Credible Rating	11	13	12	9.5

The above show that in terms of our credibility rating a federal regulatory commission is the most effective regulatory structure.

We should recognise political and practical constraints. Which regimes are more acceptable to member states? How fast and effective are the mechanisms of regulation in each regime? Questions like this pose a further question: Credibility at what price? Accepting these practical limits we therefore score the credibility function of the competing regulatory systems in terms of:

- Speed: The ability to co-ordinate policy goals across Europe, mediate between the various member states goals and make quick competition judgements.
- Flexibility: While it is important for a level playing field in a single market, the new regulatory regime must be sensitive to cultural and institutional variance within the EU.
- Jurisdictional transparency: Provide a clear understanding of the policy process, the points of appeal, who makes decisions and why. At present the European Treaty requires Regulations, Directives and decisions adopted by the EU to have accompanying statements outlining the reasoning for legislation. However, there

12 For example the Sutherland Report in 1992 expressed a need for the Commission to become more open and transparent and introduce procedures for developing regulatory awareness.

would appear to be discrepancy between the member states legal requirements - with direct consequences for business action and regulatory circumvention.

- One size fits all: How universal is the regulatory regime? Are the skills and institutional access points similar across: firms, sectors and countries?
- Political Implementation. What regulatory institutions are acceptable and more likely to be accommodated by member states?

In Table 4 we calculate the credibility cost of each regulatory regime. The scoring is as before and in addition assigns No (zero), Yes (1), Maybe (0.5), negative (-1), positive (1), Neutral (0), and Status Quo (0).

Table 4: Credibility: At What Price?

Characteristics	Current Regulatory Regime	Federal Regulatory Commission	Regulatory Agency	Regulatory Forum
Speed	Medium	Low	High	High
Flexibility	Medium	Low	High	Medium-high
Jurisdictional Transparency	Medium	High	Medium	Medium-Low
One size fits all				
Firms	No	No	Yes	Maybe
Industries	No	No	Yes	Yes
Countries	Maybe	No	Maybe	Maybe
Political Reality	Status Quo	EU -ve. States -ve	EU +ve States -ve	EU: Neutral States: Neutral
Credibility Costing Score	6.5	3	10.5	9
Aggregate Score	**17.5**	**16**	**22.5**	**18.5**

Recognising that the Commission favours delegating decision-making powers to NRAs, it is clear that new regulatory regimes must establish checks and counter balances that co-ordinate the NRA decisions and positions at the EU level. At present co-ordination relies on an informal consensus building process among the NRA and Commission. However, such an approach requires legal powers to ensure full implementation and formal bodies that provide equal access to all parties involved in the decision-making process. In terms of our study, it is apparent that the regulatory agency scores highly in terms of expertise, legitimacy, accountability and flexibility. Yet, for all its potential benefits, and pressure from the European Parliament, the Commission and member states would appear reluctant to hand over executive powers to a new institution.

Thus a formal network of co-ordinated NRAs would appear to provide the most practical and credible 'second best' solution.

5. Concluding Remarks

With ongoing liberalisation in the single market and growing competition and regulatory challenges, there are increasing demands for pan-European regulation. On the basis of our qualitative analysis we advocate that Europe will be best served by adopting an Agency regime. However, while agencies perform well in terms of our simple regulatory topology and practical application, some political and legal questions still surround them in the European context.

Viewed as part of a medium term solution we can expect EU institutions to continue to encourage some form of regulatory convergence/uniformity in member states and for NRAs to put in place the best regulatory regime for consumers in the respective countries within a broad European framework of principles. Much of this EU regulatory convergence will be initiated via the introduction of liberalization directives and Reviews (such as the 1999 Telecom Review). We can also expect the EU institutions to be more proactive in raising regulatory questions via the use of resolutions and recommendations. As David Edmonds notes: "*As competition grows and deepens, (NRA) can rely increasingly on competition law. But (we are) likely to need sectoral rules to deal with certain competition issues for some time.*"

In sum, we can expect multiple speed regulatory harmonisation across sectors and countries, as it is doubtful if one model can fit all scenarios. However, whatever the speed of change there is a need for a clear regulatory process that governments, regulators and businesses can live with. Although, European agencies may ultimately provide this structure, flexibility and expertise, current political reality would make this difficult. Few NRAs or member states would feel comfortable with this distribution of power and the European Commission would appear to favour regulatory forums in line with the concept of subsidiarity.

References

Baldwin, R. and Caves, M. (1999) *Understanding Regulation,* Oxford, Oxford University Press.

Bergman, L. Doyle, D. Gual, J. Hultrantz, L. Neven, D. Roller, L. Waverman, L (1998) *Europe's Network Industries: Conflicting Priorities.* Monitoring European Deregulation series 1, London, CEPR.

Coen, D. (1998) "The European Business Interest and the Nation State: Large-Firm lobbying in the European Union" *Journal of Public Policy*, vol. 18:1.

Dehousse, R. (1993) "Integration v regulation? On the Dynamics of Regulation in the European Community" *Journal of Common Market Studies* 383.

Dehousse, R. (1997), Regulation by networks in the EC: The role of European agencies, *Journal of European Public Policy*, Vol. 4:2.

Doern, B. and S. Wilks, (eds) *Comparative Competition Policy: National Institutions in a Global Market*, Oxford, Clarendon.

Doyle, C. (1996) "European telecommunication policy" *Journal of European Public Policy* Vol. 3:4

Ehlermann, C. (1995) "Reflections on a European Cartel Office" *Common Market Law Review,* Vol. 32

Egan M. (1997) "Regulatory Strategies, Delegation and European Market Integration" *Journal of European Public Policy* Vol. 5:3

Everson, M. (1996) The German Federal Supervisory Authority for Insurance, in: *Regulating Europe*, London Routledge 1996.

Everson, M. (1995), "Independent Agencies: Hierarchy Beaters," *European Law Journal*, Vol.1.

Hancher, L. (1996) Utilities policy and the European Union, an overview, in: *Regulatory Review* 1996, London CRI.

Heritier, A. (1996), "The Accommodation of Diversity in the European Policy-Making and its Outcomes: Regulatory policy as Patchwork" *Journal of European Public Policy*, Vol. 3.

Kreher, A. (1997), Agencies in the EC - a step towards administrative integration in Europe, *Journal of European Public Policy*, Vol. 4:2.

Levy, B and Spiller P (1994) The institutional foundations of regulatory commitment: a comparative analysis of telecommunications regulation. *Journal of Law Economics and Organisation* Vol. 10:2

Levi-Faur, D. (1999), "Governing Dutch telecommunications reform: State-Business interaction in the transformation of national policy regimes to (European) embedded policy regimes" *Journal of European Public Policy*. Vol. 6:1.

Laudati, L. (1996) The European Commission as Regulator: the uncertain pursuit of the competitive market, in G. Majone (ed.) *Regulating Europe*, London, Routledge.

Majone, G. (1994), "The rise of the Regulatory State" *West European Politics,* 17:3.

Majone, G. (1996), *Regulating Europe,* London, Routledge.

Majone, G. (1997), The new European agencies: regulation by information, *Journal of European Public Policy Vol. 4.2.*

McGowan, F. and Wallace, H. (1996) "Towards a European Regulatory State" *Journal of European Public Policy*, Vol. 3:4

Pons, J. (1999), "The Liberalisation of telecommunication in Europe and the role of the regulators" European Commission DGIV speech 12th April Rome 1999.

Radaelli, C. (1998) *Governing European regulation: The Challenges Ahead.* RSC Policy Paper, No 98/3

Shapiro, M. 1997, the problems of independent agencies in the US and the EU, *Journal of European Public Policy*, Vol. 4:2.

Stern, J. and Holder S. (1999) "Regulatory Governance: Criteria for assessing the performance of regulatory systems. An application to Asia" *Utilities Policy* Vol. 8.

Synder, F. (1993) The effectiveness of European Community Law: Institutions, processes, tools and techniques" *Modern Law Review* Vol. 56.

Thatcher, M. (1997) "Regulating the regulators: The regulatory Regime for the British Privatised Utilities" *Parliamentary Affairs*, Vol. 51:2.

Thatcher, M. (1998) "Institutions, Regulation, and Change: New Regulatory Agencies in the British Privatised Utilities." Vol. 21:1

Weiler J. (1995) "After Maastricht: Community legitimacy in post-1992 Europe" in W.J. Adams (ed.), *Singular Europe: Economy and Polity of the European Community after 1992*, Ann Arbor: University of Michigan Press.

Wilks, S. (1996) "Regulatory Compliance and capitalist diversity in Europe" in *Journal of European Public Policy*, Vol.3:4.

Wilks S., and McGowan, L. (1996) "Competition policy in the European Union: creating a federal agency? in B. Doern, and S. Wilks, (eds) *Comparative Competition Policy: National Institutions in a Global Market*. Oxford. Clarendon.

STYLES OF REGULATION: THE CHOICE OF APPROACH TO UTILITY REGULATION IN CENTRAL AND EASTERN EUROPE

Jon Stern
LBS and NERA

1. INTRODUCTION

Since 1990, the countries of Central and Eastern Europe have been under considerable pressure to develop explicit regulatory institutions. Initially, the main pressure for this policy came from the World Bank and other international lending agencies. Indeed, the requirement for an independent regulator was often included as an explicit loan condition by lending agencies. Subsequently, and in practice more importantly, there was the pressure for transparent regulation arising from the need to provide an effective basis for private investment and privatisation. More recently, there has been the impetus from desired accession to the European Union (EU) and the need to meet the terms of the relevant EU Directives.

Before 1990, in all CEE economies, the *economic regulation* of utilities (including energy, telecommunications, etc) was not at all recognised as a separate activity. It was carried out along with *policy* and the *ownership/management* of the state-owned enterprises by the relevant Government Ministries. Indeed, the regulation of eg investment and prices was not recognised as at all separate from policy or from the running or financing of the enterprises. The dominant forces involved were typically the Communist Party leadership and the senior managers of the relevant enterprises (the nomenklatura) who paid little weight to commercial factors. [1]

As a result of these factors, the CEE countries have had to start from the very beginning in developing regulatory functions for utilities – just as in the financial sector and other parts of the economy. In addition, there has been considerable competition from supporters of different regulatory models. Thus, not surprisingly, USAID assistance has tended to promote the US model of rule-based, legally-driven regulation; UK assistance and companies has tended to promote independent but less formal regulation;

---

[1] See Cave and Stern (1998) for further discussion of the pre-1990 arrangements.

Continental European countries and companies have tended to urge caution on the development of explicit, independent regulatory institutions, and so on.

Perhaps more importantly, potential foreign investors and privatisation purchasers have also been active lobbyists for their preferred style of regulation and, even more so, for their preferred degree of liberalisation. The energy and other companies involved in activities in CEE countries, not surprisingly, also tend to advocate the style of regulation of their home country. This tendency does, though, have some interesting exceptions, as we shall demonstrate below.

In consequence, we can see that, over the last decade, *CEE countries have seen a competition among external forces over the relative merits of the various different approaches to utility regulation as used in Western Europe, North America and elsewhere.*

Within the CEE countries, there have been internal pressures both to maintain the power of Ministries and to reduce their powers, particularly for line-Ministries (what were previously the sponsoring Ministries). There has also been the need to develop fair relationships with powerful foreign investors and the fear that new specialist regulatory agencies would be subject to regulatory capture. In addition, the various agencies in the CEE countries have been able to observe the debates and choices of the existing EU members as regards utility regulation and their responses to the various EU Directives.

The internal pressures have interacted in interesting and complicated ways with the external forces in the choice of regulatory style adopted. We are now seeing the results of the "regulatory design competition". Hungary and Poland now have independent energy regulators and the Czech Republic has made considerable progress in developing an Energy Law that would establish an independent regulator. Interestingly (and perhaps surprisingly), less progress has been made on establishing independent regulation for telecommunications. The reasons for this are very interesting and will be discussed later in the paper.

In consequence, we can now provide some evidence on the results of the competition between regulatory models in Central Europe. We can also identify some common patterns among options that have been chosen and point out models that have not been chosen. These issues provide the theme for this paper.

In Section 2, we discuss the main models in the main EU countries and elsewhere. In Section 3, we outline the choices of regulatory institution made in CEE countries, concentrating on energy and telecommunications in the three main Central European countries. In Section 4, we discuss the reasons for the patterns observed and, in Section 5, we compare these choices with the main models discussed in Section 2. Section 6 provides a short conclusion.

Appendix A provides some observations on regulation in CIS counties, primarily electricity regulation, including comments on EBRD (and other) regulatory league tables. The Appendix raises a number of questions prompted by the examination of CEE utility regulation, many of which are deliberately left less than fully answered. A key issue is whether and how far it is sensible to use the same definitions and criteria for describing regulatory institutions in (say) Georgia or Kazakhstan as for (say) Hungary and Poland.

Speculations on these and related topics may be of interest to some readers but are best relegated to an appendix.

2. Regulatory Models

The main models for utility regulation can be summarised as follows. The listing starts with the most ambitious in terms of autonomy and progresses through to the classic Communist framework mentioned above.

1) The US Model of Regulation

The US model of utility regulation is generally seen as the epitome of *independent* regulation, with its emphasis on specialist regulatory institutions operating within a highly *rule-based and legalistic* framework. It is explicitly *adversarial* with an emphasis on *public hearings*. The resulting structure is locked into a system of administrative law in which the courts (up to and including the Supreme Court) play a major role. Indeed, the courts and legal concerns can take over the substance of regulation as well as its form.[2]

US regulation is often perceived (particularly in the Central European countries) as a very *resource intensive system*, dominated by lawyers and requiring large numbers of lawyers and other experienced professionals (economists, accountants, etc) to make it run. Accusations of *regulatory capture* are often made about the US system. The existence of this self-contained world of well-paid regulatory professionals is again perceived in Central European countries as one reason why regulatory capture can arise.

2) The UK Model

The UK model is also a model of *independent* regulation, but based on *small, specialist regulatory Offices*. Relative to the US model, it is *less formal* in its processes and requirements. Thus, the law courts play a relatively minor role, with most appeals being handled by the Competition Commission (as successor to the Monopoly and Mergers Commission). The less legally dominated approach leads to *more rapid and less resource intensive* regulation, but provides less clearcut security to regulated companies and may be *less predictable*.

In addition, particularly from the Central European perspective, UK regulation appears to be *less divorced from the policy process* (eg the government can choose the single person regulatory office head).

---

[2] This picture is truer at the Federal level than at the state level where direct political accountability by Regulatory commissioners can lead to less pure outcomes.

3) The German Model

For electricity and gas, Germany has so far decided *not* to have a sector-specific independent regulatory agency.

For the critical issues of network access and pricing (including the requirements of the EU Electricity and Gas Directives), in Germany it is the Federal Cartel Office that carries out regulatory functions eg for dispute resolution under the Competition Law. For electricity, there is an Associations Agreement negotiated by the industry and its associations and registered with the Cartel Office. The initial version of this expired in September 1999 and a new version has recently been agreed.

Regulation of electricity distribution and retail supply (and the appropriate methodology) is still the responsibility of the Federal Ministry of Economy and the corresponding Länder agencies.[3]

The German system would seem to *require even fewer resources* and to be *less subject to dangers of regulatory capture.* It does, however, require *a strong and well-established competition agency*. For economies where the dangers of cartel behaviour by the existing players are strong, there are obvious risks of *anti-competitive behaviour* and exclusion of new entry. Indeed, many such accusations have been made against Germany and there have been some high profile court cases (eg Enron and access to Stadtwerke Ludenscheid).

For telecommunications, Germany has an independent regulatory agency (as required by the relevant EU Directives. Many observers suggest that energy will follow suit and that an electricity (or energy regulator) will be developed in the near future.

4) Ministerial Regulation – the Continental West European Model

This model is that where a government department regulates (and typically sponsors) a state-owned monopoly utility. This is the pre-1989 England and Wales model with the Department of Energy regulating the CEGB, in association with the Treasury. It was the standard West European model in the period 1960-90 and was adopted in many countries.

The archetype of this approach is conventionally taken as the relationship between EdF and the French government where EdF was "regulated" under a Planning Contract (Contrat du Plan) with the French government. However, the French authorities have published a draft Electricity Act, which is proceeding (slowly) through the legislature. This draft Act provides for an independent electricity regulator responsible for network access and pricing. The French government has already established an independent telecommunications regulator. It remains to be seen, however, how independent the French electricity regulator will be in view of the dominant position of EdF in the French electricity market.

---

[3] Australia has a similar system, with the ACCC responsible for economic regulation of electricity, particularly network access and pricing. The States are responsible for customer prices and technical aspects of regulation. Again, there is a voluntarily agreed network code, approved by the ACCC.

Perhaps more relevantly for CEE countries, Austria currently retains the key features of the Continental European model. There is no independent regulatory agency and, for electricity, the regulation of all aspects of network access and pricing fall to the Ministry of Economy. The Competition Authority is also a department of the Ministry of Economy.

For CEE countries, this model represents least change on their pre-1989 arrangements. It can also be defended as the one *appropriate to commercialised, publicly-owned utilities operating in a market economy*. It continues to link *policy and regulation* and readily allows the continuation of *continued explicit and implicit subsidies and cross-subsidies*.[4] It is also the model that is most conducive of *protection of domestic incumbent companies*. However, although well-suited to building-up universal network and supply coverage (the policy objectives in the past), this model is not well-suited to the current tasks of increasing efficiency, reducing costs and supporting the introduction of competition.

5) Central and East European Communist Countries Pre-1989

Regulation of utilities here can be taken as a heavily distorted variant of the West European model. The worst distortions arose from the fact that the utilities did not operated in a commercialised way. In particular, their investments were largely determined by the Central Plan and the Plan physical output targets, and were funded out of the central budget. Tariffs were at best only intended to cover operating costs in toto, included little or no depreciation or profit element and households were heavily cross-subsidised by industrial customers.

By 1989, this model was discredited and the question was what should replace it. Apart from the strongest opponents of reform (eg Belarus), it was clear that this model was no longer viable. Hence, the question was whether to go for the minimal change option of the West European Ministry-regulation option (model 4) or for one of the more radical options.

In practice, as we shall see, at least for electricity, the answers to the choice between Model 4 or one of Models 1-3 primarily reflected attitudes to:

(i) the desired degree of liberalisation and competition;
(ii) the chosen role for private investment; and
(iii) the degree to which CEE governments wanted to continue to allow regulation to be affected by policy concerns.

The choice between Model 1, 2 or 3 reflected additional factors, which we will discuss in Section 4.

---

[4] EdF has frequently been accused of benefiting from hidden subsidies. It has consistently defended itself strongly against such accusations and none of the investigations by eg EU bodies has found against EdF.

3. REGULATORY CHOICES IN THE COUNTRIES OF CENTRAL AND EAST EUROPE

In this section, we will mainly discuss the regulatory choices made in the electricity industries of CEE countries, as this is the area where there has been most activity. We will, however, briefly discuss telecommunications where, perhaps surprisingly given EU developments, there has been less progress on regulation, even though there has been much more liberalisation and privatisation activity than in electricity or gas.

The discussion will concentrate on the three main reforming Central European economies - Hungary, the Czech Republic and Poland. There have, though, been some interesting recent developments in, Bulgaria and Romania, which we will also discuss.

On paper, there appears to be considerable development of regulatory institutions in some of the CIS countries. However, it is far from clear whether the practice of regulation in the very difficult economic circumstances of countries like Georgia or Kazakhstan corresponds at all closely to what one would expect in Central Europe, let alone Western Europe. We will discuss this issue briefly at the end of this section.

3.1 The Central European Countries: Electricity

3.1.1 Hungary

Hungary was the first CEE country to pass a law introducing an independent regulator in the energy sector. The Hungarian Energy Office (HEO) was established to regulate electricity and gas under electricity and gas laws enacted in 1994.

The HEO is responsible for issuing and amending licences. On prices, it establishes pricing criteria and rules, but it is the Minister of Industry who actually decides the prices. The Hungarian government has more than once over-ruled HEO tariff change recommendations. Similarly, it is the Ministry and not the HEO that approves or makes the formal proposals to the Government or the Parliament on power station approvals.

The degree of independence of the HEO is limited by the following features:

- There is no fixed term for the HEO's Chief Director;
- The Chief Director and other directors are appointed by the Minister of Industry and Trade but not with a fixed term of office;
- There are no specified dismissal (or appointment) criteria or procedures for the Chief Director or the other directors;
- The HEO does not have an independent revenue source. Its budget is part of the Ministry of Industry's budget;
- The pay of HEO staff is fixed on Civil Service pay scales;

- The HEO has no rights to issue general decrees; and
- There are no specific appeals mechanisms eg via the national competition agency or the courts, although all regulatory decisions will be subject to general appeal rights under Hungarian law.

From the above, it can reasonably be argued that the HEO is essentially a Ministry regulator masquerading as a UK style regulator. A more charitable interpretation is that it is a UK-style regulatory office but with heavily circumscribed powers. It certainly has none of the procedural or other characteristics of the US system.

Certainly, foreign investors who have purchased share stakes in the Hungarian electricity and gas distribution companies and in electricity generation companies have regularly and increasingly vociferously voiced their disappointment with the Hungarian energy regulatory system.[5] Both EdF and Gaz de France (GdF) have been among the vocal complainers. However, this dissatisfaction with the regulatory safeguards did not prevent a sizeable number of foreign energy companies from submitting bids in the 1998 generation tender.

In terms of the typology of the previous section, the HEO has few if any of the features of the US or German models. The aspects of "new-style" regulation adopted owe most to the UK office system. In particular, Hungary (like other CEE countries) has adopted a *licensing* approach, with licences for fixed periods setting out the rights and obligations of the regulated companies. The licenses are the key document in the monitoring and enforcement of regulation. This approach has been adopted in spite of the legal difficulties involved in developing complex regulatory licences in a framework of Continental Law where simple permit licences are the norm.[6]

In practice, however, the HEO has found that its powers are highly circumscribed and that real regulatory power remains with the government. This includes the issue of how the EU Electricity and Gas Directives will be implemented in Hungary.

3.1.2 Poland

Poland's energy regulator, the Office of Energy Regulation (OER), was established by the 1997 Energy Law. It is in operation, but its first tariff ruling isppears not to be due until 2000. Indeed, the OER regulatory activities so far seem to be very low profile and, unlike the HEO, not to have achieved much publicity. However, this may be because there has so far been very little privatisation in the Polish electricity industry and even less involvement of foreign investors.[7]

---

[5] This is an ongoing and fascinating story whose various episodes are well-chronicled in the FT East European Energy Newsletter.

[6] France and Francophone countries usually use Franchise Concessions where the associated Cahiers de Charges cover the material usually included in UK-style licences. There are no licenses or equivalents in US or German regulatory systems.

[7] Poland has considerable amounts of spare generating capacity, albeit much of it inefficient and/or environmentally unsound, and is exporting cheap electricity eg to the Czech Republic..

The Polish Energy Law establishes a very UK-like regulator. The OER has far more of the attributes of a formally independent regulator than its Hungarian equivalent. Among the key features of its governance are:

- The Chairman of the OER is the legal person who makes regulatory decisions.
- He/she has a 5 year fixed period appointment and can only be recalled within their term of office for serious incapacity or (specified) misdemeanours;
- The OER is financed out of licence fees;
- The staff of the OER are not paid on Civil Service pay scales but on rates decided after "consideration" of pay scales in the fuel and energy sector; and
- Appeals on OER decisions can be lodged before the Anti-monopoly Court while the OER is explicitly subject to the Administrative Proceedings Act.

In addition, the OER is explicitly responsible for regulatory *decisions* not just on *granting licences*[8], but also on *prices and investment*. (For the latter, it has to approve "development plans".) The OER can also decide whether or not there is sufficient competition in any market segment to allow the ending of tariff regulation.

There are, however, a number of ways in which the powers of the OER are potentially reduced. The main ones are as follows:

(i) The OER cannot decide its own procedures or organisational structure (and hence the number of staff). These are laid down in an Ordinance issued by the Prime Minister. Similarly, it is a Prime Ministerial Ordinance that sets out OER staff pay principles.

(ii) The OER is obliged to carry out energy regulation "in compliance with the assumptions of state energy policy".

(iii) The OER does not appear to have the power to issue general decrees or guidance. Thus, licence exemption criteria are laid down by the Ministry of Economy.

(iv) Pricing criteria in the Law are very loosely defined – there is a reference to prices covering "reasonably justified costs", but there is no definition of these. Nor is there any requirement that prices should allow the expectation of a reasonable rate of return or even that they ensure the financial viability of regulated enterprises. Indeed, there is no reference to anything other than operating costs or "costs of development" in the coverage of reasonably justified costs.

(v) More importantly, it is *not* the OER that lays down the criteria for price regulation. This is to be done by an Ordinance issued by "the Minister of the Economy, in consultation with the Ministry of Finance, and after taking advice from the Chairman of the OER".[9] Other key methodological issues are also to be set out in *Ministry* Ordinances.

---

[8] The official English translation of the Energy Law uses the word "concession", but it is in fact a UK-style licence not a French-style franchise concession.

[9] Polish Energy Law, April 1997, Article 46.

It is still unclear whether the Government will actively use its powers to limit the autonomy of the OER through its powers (and duties) with regard (a) to the key methodological secondary legislation; and, (b) through laying down energy policy.

The primary law ducks many of the key regulatory issues (eg on OER procedures, tariff regulation criteria, etc). If it chose to do so, the Government could use its secondary legislation powers so as greatly to limit the autonomy of the OER. On the other hand, the Government could effectively delegate these powers to the OER. For instance, it could choose to request the OER to prepare the key Ordinances and wave them through. Similarly, it could choose to give only very general policy principles.

The outcome of this process is still very unclear. The only straw in the wind is that the OER Chairman appointed towards the end of the term of the previous Government remains active and in post. This shows a degree of commitment to good regulatory practice and continuity.

Summarising, the Polish OER *looks* essentially like a UK-style regulatory office and, in practice, could turn out to act like one. However, it could, if the Government so chose, be rather closer to an out-house Ministerial regulator with limited autonomy. In any event, it has few if any of the characteristics of either the US or the German styles of utility regulation.

3.1.3 The Czech Republic

The current basis for energy sector regulation in the Czech Republic is a law enacted in 1994 under which the Ministry of Economy is responsible for all aspects of regulation except price regulation. Price regulation is the responsibility of the Ministry of Finances under a general price regulation law, enacted in 1991.

The 1994 Energy Act was passed hurriedly to fill a legal vacuum. Its defects became clear very rapidly and there have been discussions on amending or replacing it for some years. The pressure for a new energy law grew substantially with the need to provide for the incorporation of provisions of the EU Electricity and Gas Directives into Czech Law to meet accession requirements.

The 1994 Act reflected the attitude of the Klaus government towards regulation. Prime Minister Klaus was adamantly opposed to specialist regulatory agencies, which he believed were, in the context of Transition Economies, bound to be subject to complete regulatory capture. He expressed this hostility strongly and publicly. On the other hand, the Ministry of Finance was seen as the general and impartial guardian of the public interest.[10] However, the Ministry of Finance was not equipped to cover other aspects of utility regulation so, for electricity, regulatory responsibilities were divided between the Ministry of Finance and the Ministry of Economy.

In addition, Prime Minister Klaus continued to fight publicly as well as privately against increases in energy prices to households. It was clear that the development of an

10 It is not co-incidental that Mr Klaus had been Minister of Finance in the CSFR Government before the CSFR split into separate countries at the end of 1992.

independent regulatory agency was part of a programme which included substantial price increases (particularly to households) and privatisation. But, the only privatisation allowed in the energy sector under the Klaus Government was the 1992 30% voucher privatisation.[11] No sales of strategic share stakes or IPOs were allowed in the electricity or gas industries (unlike in telecommunications).

In addition, the Czech progress on energy price rebalancing (ie raising household energy prices towards economic costs) has also been significantly less in the Czech Republic than in Hungary, Poland, or some Baltic and Balkan countries. At end-1997, household electricity prices in the Czech Republic were 3.9 US cents/kWh as compared to 6-7 cents in Romania, Latvia, Hungary and Poland and over 13 cents in the EU. Household electricity prices remain some way below operating costs (4-5 cents/kWh. The slow progress on price reform has become the major impediment to further privatisation and liberalisation of the Czech network energy industries.[12]

Hence, it is not surprising that pressures to unify regulation and establish a separate specialist regulator came to nothing under the Klaus Government. The continued political unwillingness to sanction household energy price increases has continued under the Socialist-led government that took office in 1997. However, the new Government has come out publicly in favour of an independent energy regulator and expects to present a new Draft Energy Act to the Czech Parliament by early-2000. This new Act will provide for (i) an independent energy regulator and (ii) the incorporation of relevant EU energy legislation (including the liberalisation elements of the Electricity and Gas Directives) into Czech law.

The style of regulation that has existed up to now in the Czech Republic is clearly a minimum change on pre-1989 arrangements where regulatory issues are clearly and fully subordinated to policy issues – both energy policy and also prices policy. The development was less than even to the West European Ministerial model of regulation, as there remained significant limits on the degree of commercialisation of the energy companies.

The position began to change in 1998 with the establishment of a separate Regulatory Department within the Ministry of Industry and Trade. The Director of the Regulatory Department reports directly to the Minister and is the key interface with the Ministry of Finance on energy prices, preparing the proposals for changes in regulated prices. In addition, it is the regulatory Department and its Director who have been leading the process to prepare the new Energy Act.

The proposed regulatory arrangements for electricity and gas in the Czech Republic are not dissimilar to those for Poland. Again, the intention is to have an independent agency with a Chairman, protected against arbitrary dismissal and protected funding

---

11 Distribution companies had some of their shares transferred to Municipalities and private investors (particularly foreign energy companies) have since purchased some of the Municipally-owned shares. This process is called "wild privatisation". To stop it, the current Socialist-led government has used CEZ and Transgas, the dominant electricity and gas companies to repurchase these shares. This backdoor renationalisation seems likely to cause some interesting regulatory and privatisation conflicts.

12 See Stern and Davis (1998), EBRD Transition Report (1998).

(from licence fees). The regulator would issue licences and be responsible for price regulation.

There will clearly be major debate about the precise boundaries of responsibility between the Ministry of Industry and Trade and the new regulatory agency. The proposals that have been under discussion in 1999 would, in some respects, provide more regulatory autonomy than the Polish Energy Law. For instance, under the current proposals,

(i) the regulator would have powers to issue general decrees and decisions; and
(ii) it would be the regulator who would lay down and issue pricing principles and methodologies.

But, current proposals, as in Poland, relegate some key issues for private investors to secondary legislation.

It remains to be seen where the outcome arises in the draft law, let alone the eventually enacted law. Nevertheless, in terms of the *style* of regulation, the Czech Republic again seems to be opting for a model that appears to be that of the UK office, but retains many of the attributes of the West European Ministerial regulation model. As in other Central European countries, this appears to reflect the ambivalence over early moves to liberalisation, over the introduction of genuine competition and, in particular, to the potential role of powerful foreign investors in the energy industries. We will discuss this further in Section 4 below.

Again, we see no evidence that the US-legally dominated model holds any attractions or, perhaps more surprisingly, of any moves towards adopting the German model – with one interesting exception.

The exception concerns some Ministry of Finance arguments for their opposition to a specialist energy regulator. The Ministry of Finance has, on occasion, suggested that Ministry of Finance price regulation plus general competition policy oversight would be a good model for the Czech Republic. They have, secondly claimed that this would correspond to the successful German regulatory system.

One problem with this approach is that Ministry of Finance price regulation is far more practical if there are few companies and prices to regulate – for instance one or more vertically integrated monopolies. It makes much less sense if there is considerable competition in generation and/or supply and many companies. But, the Government view is to encourage competition and the Ministry of Finance has argued the case for competition rather than regulation to the extent of suggesting that the establishment of an independent regulator could impede the development of competition. Nevertheless, these arguments seem to be increasingly left behind and the case for a UK-style regulator currently seems to be gaining ground.

3.2 Central Europe – Telecommunications

So far, none of the three main Central European countries has a fully independent telecommunications regulator.

Under a 1993 Act, Hungary established a Communication Authority. However, like the energy regulator, the Ministry retains decision-making powers on tariffs and shares the responsibility with the Authority on interconnection rates and frequency allocation. The Head of the Authority reports to the Minister of Transport and Communications.

In the Czech Republic, the Czech Telecommunication Office was set up under the Telecommunications Act of 1992. It is, however, a Department within the Ministry of Transport and Communications and wholly financed from the general budget. The position is similar to that for energy, except that the regulatory reform proposals that have so far been circulated seem not to involve creating an independent regulator with significant powers.

In Poland, telecommunications regulation is still carried out by the relevant Ministry, but a new telecommunications law is being prepared for presentation to the parliament by the end of 1999.

The lack of development of independent regulation for telecommunications is, at first sight, surprising for two main reasons.

The first reason is that, in general, reform has been faster in telecommunications than in energy. We now find competing mobile operators, competition in value added services, privatisation of major shares of the incumbent fixed-line operator (Hungary and the Czech Republic) and some limited competition in fixed line services (Hungary and Poland).

The second reason is that the EU Telecommunications Directive, unlike the Energy Directives, explicitly require an independent regulator – albeit, *a regulator independent of the incumbent fixed line telephone company*. This is consistent with having a Ministry regulator. However, under the Directives, the conditions under which the regulator must operate are quite stringent and so most EU countries have adopted a telecommunications regulator independent of government and reporting to the parliament. The list of countries adopting this includes France, Italy, Netherlands – and both Austria and Germany.

In terms of style of regulation, in CEE countries, we have so far seen Ministry-based regulators, but the signs are that, if there were to be a second stage of reform, that would most likely take them in the direction of UK-style regulatory offices, operating license-based regulatory systems. This, however, reflects developments in the Continental European members of the EU.

We discuss in more detail in Section 4.2 and in the Conclusions why CEE counties have so far been able to make extensive progress in telecommunications reform without an explicit regulator.

One recent significant development affecting the development of regulation in CEE countries is the EU programme for "twinning" regulators for EU countries with regulators in potential accession countries. So far, this appears primarily to have affected telecoms, but it is likely to spread to other industries. Interestingly, Poland has chosen to twin with OFTEL and the Swedish telecoms regulator while the Czech Republic has chosen to twin with the German regulator. This programme may well become important in the future both for disseminating a central EU view on appropriate regulatory developments and the perspectives of existing EU members. Indeed, as the twinning is carried out by competitive tender, so the programme could well continue the competition between models of regulation in a new guise.

3.3 Other CEE Countries – Electricity

Some other CEE countries have established more or (usually less) embryonic electricity and/or energy regulators. Latvia and Lithuania are examples. However, they are very small countries where regulation effectively has to be "umbrella" regulation of all the major utility services. As such, and given the inherent problem of genuinely separating regulation from policy and management in small countries, they are rather less interesting for lessons on the style of regulation.

In recent months, however, Bulgaria and, in particular, Romania have taken major steps forward that raise interesting perspectives on the choice of regulatory style.

In *Bulgaria*, there is a new regulatory agency called the State Commission for Energy and Energy Efficiency (SCEEE). It has 7 members. The State Agency for Energy and Energy Efficiency is a separate body responsible for energy policy (including restructuring, privatisation and investment). The two new agencies were established in a law finally enacted in July 1999.[13]

The SCEEE is limited in its powers. For instance, it sits under the authority of the Council of Ministers, it can only make recommendations on tariffs and prices and the Council of Ministers sets the regulations for granting licences. This is all rather like the Hungarian energy regulator. However, there are two key differences:

(i) For electricity, it introduces mandatory third party access to transmission *and* distribution systems. (Poland has the former but not the latter. Hungary and the Czech Republic have neither.)

(ii) The style of regulation incorporates some significant US elements eg the regulatory agency is a *Commission* not an *Office*. In addition, sittings of the commission will normally be in public, but there is the right to hold closed sittings.[14]

In *Romania*, the Government has established an independent electricity and heat regulator, the NRAE. This was done by an Emergency Ordinance issued in late 1998. The intention is that the Ordinance will be replaced by an Act, drafts of which have been prepared but not yet enacted.

The NRAE looks, from the 5 page Ordinance, to be a classic UK-style independent regulatory office. Thus, it is headed by a President who has a fixed term and cannot be easily dismissed; it is responsible for decisions on all aspects of regulation (including prices and tariffs); it has budgetary independence; it is responsible for setting pricing

---

[13] See FT East European Energy Newsletter July 1999, pp19-20.

[14] According to the FT EEE Newsletter report, the pressures for independence and for open meetings came primarily from the World Bank. It will be interesting to see what happens in practice, particularly when World Bank and IMF surveillance of Bulgaria is relaxed.

methodologies, etc. On paper, the NRAE is, potentially (depending on the detailed provisions in the law), much more radically independent than any other CEE regulator.

The other interesting feature is that the NRAE is obliged to work jointly with the Competition Office on price regulation. Both the "calculation approach" for regulation of natural monopoly elements and the actual setting of intermediate and final prices. Indeed, on these issues, the NRAE acts "upon advice" of the Competition Office. Other than the use of the competition agency for appeals in Poland, this appears to be the only extant example of a significant role for competition agencies in utility regulation in CEE countries.[15]

For both Bulgaria and Romania, the question of how these agencies will work in practice is a major one. They are both countries where reform has lagged and where ambitious plans have not been followed through or have failed to deliver the expected results, for one reason or another. They are also countries where the commercial and legal frameworks are under-developed and also where the political and institutional structures are not obviously geared to the separation of powers and functions - an issue at the core of independent regulatory theory and practice.

It is clear that external pressures have been critical for Bulgaria and Romania in the regulatory choices made. This raises the questions: (a) whether the reforms will be fully implemented; (b) whether they will "stick"; and, (c) how far they will operate as their domestic and foreign advocates intend. The Philippines and various Latin American countries have in the past enacted regulatory frameworks closely modelled on the US model. However, in practice, they operate very differently and often very unsatisfactorily.[16]

On the other hand, both countries desperately need private and foreign investment to help refurbish and develop their electricity industries and both are heavily dependent on IMF and World Bank programmes. The governments of both also (a) currently seem to be serious about unbundling their electricity industries and introducing competition and (b) very committed to taking the necessary steps to be eligible to join the EU. Effective reform of the electricity industry (and other utilities) with a functioning, transparent regulatory system would undoubtedly help in this.

We will discover in due course which of these sets of forces is the more powerful.

The initial developments in Bulgaria are very discouraging. The Bulgarian Government voted in Spring 2000 to dismiss all but one of the SCEEE Commissioners less than one month after it had completed its first major task. The 1999 Law states that Commissioners can only be dismissed for serious misdemeanours. Nevertheless, the Bulgarian Government has dismissed the five Commissioners without giving any reason – and the Commissioners have accepted their dismissal without fighting it. One Commissioner, Slavtcho Neykov was reported as saying that it was not his position to

---

15 See Government of Romania Emergency Ordinance for the establishment, organisation and operation of the Regulation Authority in the field of energy, 1998.

16 A key question is whether the courts are reliable. All regulatory systems – but particularly US-style regulatory systems - are vulnerable to corruption in the law courts. See Stern and Holder (1999) and the references cited therein.

criticise the decisions of his superiors.[17] So much for the commitment of the Bulgarian Government to independent regulation and the enforcement of its new energy law.

4. Reasons for CEE Utility Regulatory Choices

4.1 Electricity

Considering electricity on its own, it seems that the main determinant of the regulatory choices made by the Central European countries is the *degree of liberalisation* chosen. Hence, the most independent regulatory agency for electricity is that in Poland, the country where the network elements have been most clearly separated from generation and where there are large numbers (over 30) of generation and of distribution companies. Similarly, Romania's policy seems to be strongly competitive with a high degree of liberalisation. This again fits with the chosen regulatory model of a strongly independent regulator of the UK type.

Conversely, the Czech Republic has been slow hesitant about introducing independent regulation. It is also the country that has done least to separate generation from transmission[18] and, in CEZ, has the most traditional-style electricity company. CEZ is still 70% state-owned and appears not to have given up its ambitions to regain control of the distribution companies.[19]

Hungary is in an intermediate position. It is the one Central European country that has significantly privatised generation and distribution. It had previously established reasonable numbers of separate generation and distribution companies. But, MVM, the transmission company, has so far managed to maintain the ownership and management of the large nuclear plant of Paks, even though the transmission licence specifically prohibits the transmission company from operating in generation. Indeed, MVM appears not to have given up its ambitions to be active in generation in the Hungarian market.

Hence, both the Czech and Hungarian electricity industries remain dominated by powerful, state-owned companies which are seen as the basis for building up national champions and limiting the power and influence of large foreign energy companies. Hence, it is not surprising that there are mixed feelings towards a strongly liberalising approach – or towards independent regulatory agencies with real powers.

In addition, these attitudes are accompanied by a desire to build-up a local capitalism and an inherited corporatist tradition[20] that predates Communism. These are shared with

---

17 See FT East European Energy Report, June 2000, p 32.

18 CEZ is currently in the process of separating transmission (but not dispatch) into a separate company from generation.

19 CEZ has acted for the Czech Government in buying-up distribution company shares that Municipalities had sold to outside interests so that the Government can regain control of the privatisation process. In so doing, CEZ made it clear that they hoped that they would not be excluded from the privatisation process. See FT East European Energy Newsletter July 1999.

20 The corporatist reference here includes what political scientists classify as "statism" (as in France) as well as corporatism involving tripartite relations between government, large firms and unions (as found in Austria and Germany).

other Continental European countries – Austria and Germany as well as France. None of these three countries have been or are at the forefront of electricity liberalisation or of the establishment of independent regulatory bodies.

A particular issue here is the attitude towards *new entrants*. Corporatist (and statist) models of organisation present a series of potentially high hurdles for new entry. Conversely, separating policy from regulation and developing independent and separate regulation is usually (and rightly) seen as encouraging towards new entry. In electricity, new entry typically refers to generation although it can also affect wholesale and retail supply and trading activities. Hence, for countries with either surplus and/or high cost generating capacity, openness to new entry is a real threat to incumbent producers. In consequence, given the links between foreign investment and new entry, it is not surprising that major pushes to establishing an independent regulator have arisen in CEE countries have arisen when they have realised the imperative to bring in foreign capital and recognised the implications in terms of attitudes towards new entry.

4.2 Electricity Prices

The key point about the introduction of effective economic regulation in CEE and CIS countries is that it involves substantial *increases* in electricity and other utility service prices, particularly in household prices. This is in contrast to Latin America, much of Asia (including China but excluding India) and some of Africa where commercialisation, liberalisation and competition plus regulation are leading to *reductions* in prices. Of course, in EU countries, the various electricity reform programmes plus regulation have led to reductions in prices (viz the UK) or are now doing so (as in Germany).

In CEE countries, the government's attitude towards prices, particularly household prices, seems to be an important explanatory factor in whether or not countries are prepared to accept an independent regulator. Countries where governments are most unwilling to accept increases in prices are also likely to be those least willing to accept an independent regulatory agency.

Hungary's household electricity price in 1989 was already rather higher than elsewhere in Central Europe. Poland has a government that has been more prepared to raise household prices as part of its economic reform programme. In addition, the faster and more sustained growth of GDP and living standards in Poland mean that such increases are more sustainable in both economic and political terms. These are the Central European countries that have made most progress in introducing effective and independent regulation. However, it is worth noting that the Hungarian government's interventions in the regulatory process have been most notable in the area of energy prices in general and household prices in particular.

The conjecture set out above is also supported by the fact that the Czech government and the Slovak government (particularly under Meciar) have been noticeably hostile to price increases, especially to households, and they have also made much least progress among CEE countries in establishing independent regulatory institutions. Similarly, it is no co-incidence that Romania and Bulgaria have instituted major regulatory reforms at the point where economic circumstances (and the international financial institutions) have forced them to implement significant energy price increases to households.

Average CEE & CIS Household Electricity Tariffs 1997

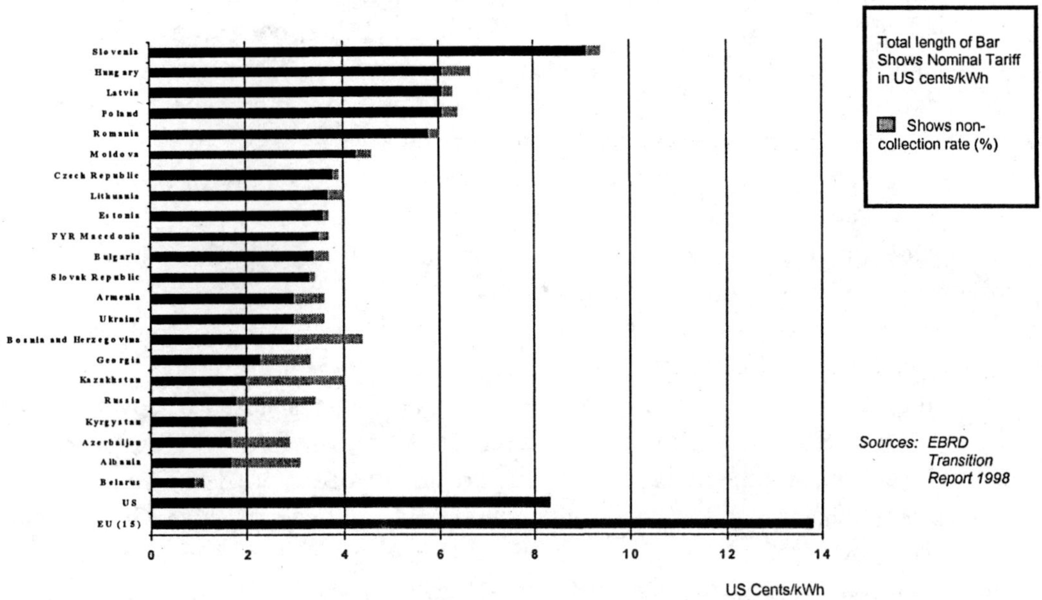

Nevertheless, the story is not quite so simple. The highest CEE electricity prices are in Slovenia, a country (albeit a small country) which is only now introducing regulatory reform. Russia and Kazakhstan have energy regulators (of a kind) but, as shown in the table above, have relatively low electricity prices, although the Kazakh *nominal* price is comparable to that in much of CEE countries. That, however, again raises the question of whether and how far the regulatory agencies in the CIS counties are comparable to those in Western and Central Europe.

4.2.1 Political and Legal Arrangements

Separating regulation from policy and establishing independent regulatory institutions requires:

- Effective political and economic institutions;
- Separation of powers, particularly between the executive and the legal system;
- A well-functioning legal system and sound courts;
- A good commercial law framework and some competition policy basis;

- A supply of well qualified staff able to carry out the various functions; and
- A functional commercial framework.

In short, considerable sophistication is required in political and legal thinking and practice, particularly as these concern commercial activity.

This line of argument concerning the existence and sustainability of independent regulatory institutions is the one emphasised by Pablo Spiller and his co-authors. Indeed, the 1998 paper by Bergara, Henisz and Spiller find that, controlling for other factors, well-defined and credible political institutions are sizeable and statistically significant predictors of regulatory effectiveness world-wide (as proxied by generation capacity) and that the best single predictor is judicial independence.

Elsewhere, I have emphasised the importance of the supply of potential regulatory staff as a key factor in whether or not countries can (and are willing to) establish independent regulatory agencies.[21] This is particularly important for the small countries, of which the CEE and the CIS has many.

In the context of this paper, it is clear that the degree of political and legal sophistication and effectiveness is important. The core Central European countries score more highly on these factors than the Balkan or Baltic states. Moreover, Poland and Hungary both made significant advances in these areas before 1989 eg the abolition of central planning and the incorporation into Polish law of the pre-1939 Commercial Code. That was not the case in the CSFR, let alone the Balkan or Baltic states. In addition, there is likely to be some correlation between the degree of political and legal sophistication and the potential supply of human capital resources of the type needed to support independent regulation.

The real difference, however, is with countries like Ukraine, Kazakhstan and the other new CIS states. Under Communism, these were not only controlled from Moscow, but they had never previously existed as independent functioning states with their own political and legal systems and structures. Unlike the core Central European countries, they had little commercial or industrial history except that under the USSR. Hence, it is not surprising that introducing effective regulation (in general and not just for utilities) creates such severe difficulties - both in providing legitimacy to the regulatory institutions and to finding the necessary trained human resources.

Leaving aside the new CIS countries, the political and legal problems of introducing genuinely independent regulation in the various CEE countries are relevant for the fear that independent regulatory institutions will be subject to regulatory capture. Such fears are particularly manifest with electricity, which (together with coal mining) was such a crucial and well-protected part of Communist states. This fear is more relevant, the less developed are the intermediate political and social institutions of a "civil society"

The factors discussed above are not unimportant in helping explain the differences between CEE countries approaches to regulation, but, as will become clear in the next section on telecommunications, seem to me less important than some of the underlying economic factors.

---

21 See Stern (1994).

4.3 Telecommunications

At the start of Section 4.1 on electricity, we suggested that it was the *degree of liberalisation* that was the main determinant of the progress in introducing explicit and independent regulatory institutions. This seems eminently plausible. However, it does not apply at all to telecommunications where considerable liberalisation, competition and privatisation have already been introduced but there are no currently functioning independent CEE telecom regulators. How can this difference be explained?

The answer seems that the high demand for telecom services coupled with the low penetration rate[22] provide the basis for profitable activities and system expansion that can proceed in the absence of an independent regulator. Given the economies of scale available, the potential for the sales of new services and the general excess demand for lines and service, a regulator is not needed even to support foreign investment in fixed or mobile telecoms *provided that governments do not intervene in a damaging way*. So far no CEE government has done so, not least because the development of an efficient and modern telecoms industry is so crucial to the economic development of the countries. In this context, all CEE countries seem effectively to have recognised the need for new entry, typically involving foreign firms, even if this is combined with some transitional protection of local incumbents.

The relative neglect under Communism of "unproductive" telecoms relative to "essential industry" electricity has thus greatly eased the regulatory needs for telecoms. As pointed out in Cave and Stern (1998), the potentially high profits available means that there has been no shortage of potential strategic partners, of bidders for franchises, or of potential privatisation purchasers.

Unlike electricity, where CEE demand has been stagnant or slow-growing, the buoyancy of telecom demand has been so far been sufficient to obviate the need for explicit regulatory institutions to support strong private and foreign investment growth. As a result, there is now the development of competing fixed as well as mobile services with the real possibility of competition between networks eg at the local loop as well as the trunk network level. This is not the case for electricity.[23]

In fact, the lack of development of independent regulatory agencies for telecommunications in Central Europe and many other Transition Economies is not so surprising.

The reasons why are as follows:

(i) There is strong demand for telecom services, particularly among business users.

(ii) There is a willingness to pay because services are being expanded in terms of range and quality.

(iii) The combination of (i) and (ii) means that the incumbent companies are profitable and can readily finance new investment. In addition, because of strong

---

22 9-17 fixed lines per 100 inhabitants in 1991/92 rising to 15-24 per 100 in 1995 as compared to 50 lines per 100 inhabitants in the UK in 1995.

23 See Stern (1999) forthcoming for further discussion of the role of demand factors. See also EBRD Transition Report 1998.

growth in demand they can improve labour productivity without requiring large-scale redundancies.

(iv) Foreign investment is needed to allow for the introduction of modern telecom technologies and marketing techniques.

(v) Competition (primarily via mobile) and privatisation (primarily via sales of strategic stakes to foreign partners) is supported by the growth in demand and willingness to pay by customers. This also brings in foreign capital and expertise.

The consequence is that there is *less need* for regulation to ensure the effective working of telecoms markets, to foster new entry or to support privatisation. Independent regulatory agencies might help improve the economic and technical efficiency of services, but, in Transition Economies, they do not seem critical for supporting private investment and competition in telecommunications. For electricity, gas and water, effective and independent regulatory agencies do seem critical to support commercialisation, private investment and competition (as has also been found in West European countries).[24]

5. Comparison with OECD Regulatory Models

In Section 2, we outlined four main models that were competitors for the design of CEE and CIS regulatory systems. These were:

1) The US rule and court based model
2) The UK regulatory office model
3) The German competition agency based model
4) The Continental European Ministry-based model

Considering the CEE countries, *the US model has not been adopted anywhere.* Only Bulgaria has even in principle adopted any of the key features of the US model for electricity and then only in a relatively minor way (the use of public hearings).

The main reasons for this seem to be as follows:

There is dislike of entrenching a permanent, rule based system at this stage of transition;

- The human resources available to run such a system are simply not available and have better uses;
- The model depends on a well-entrenched 200 year old Constitution which enforces considerable separation of powers. These look particularly alien in CEE countries;
- There is resistance to a heavily law (and lawyer) driven system which is accompanied by under-developed and inadequate commercial law frameworks and courts;
- It requires a more complete withdrawal by governments from the utility sector than these countries (or other European countries) are willing to accept.

[24] See Cave and Stern (1998) and Stern (1999) for further elaboration of these arguments.

The German competition agency model has also not been adopted in any CEE country. This is at first sight somewhat surprising given the German (and German company) involvement in Central Europe. However, there are good reasons why this is so. The main ones seem to be:

- Unlike the German Federal Cartel Office, competition agencies in CEE countries are relatively weak and not yet well-established or well-staffed. CEE competition agencies are more like fair trade enforcement agencies than West European competition, merger and monopoly agencies;[25]
- Unlike Germany, there is no established tradition of competition law or of using competition policy to achieve micro-economic policy objectives or in regulation;
- This model depends on voluntary agreements between the various companies and major consumers which may well be difficult to achieve in CEE countries;
- The model is very corporatist and inimical to new entry or foreign investment. All CEE countries recognise the need to reduce somewhat the power of their incumbent utilities and bring in foreign investment; and
- The model is under pressure in its own home countries and does not apply in Germany for telecoms, where there is a powerful, interventionist and independent regulator.

The Continental West European Ministry based regulator is used for telecoms (eg in Hungary and the Czech Republic) but has not been adopted anywhere for electricity other than by default. In essence, electricity regulation has tended to develop along the lines of UK-style offices in those countries where regulatory reform has been or is being undertaken (Hungary, Poland, Czech Republic, Bulgaria and Romania). Otherwise, the regulatory arrangements are more the continuation of Communist arrangements rather than the specific choice of the Continental West European model. This is particularly so for slow-reforming CIS countries. Slovakia also fits this view although with some characteristics of the Continental model that are necessary for supporting a more developed commercial and market utility sector.

One reason for this is that Ministries in CEE countries are relatively weak and under-staffed, particularly in less developed CEE and CIS countries. The key linkages under Communism were between the Communist Party and the top management of key companies. In the 1990s, Ministry officials are not well-paid and the best of them have many - rather more attractive - alternative employment opportunities.

In consequence, the UK regulatory office model seems to be the main model chosen for electricity by the active reformers. In particular, it is very noticeable how the UK licence framework has become the dominant regulatory instrument in CEE countries for telecoms as well as electricity and gas. The licensing model is not used for US or in most Continental West European countries and does not easily fit into the framework of Continental Law.

The dominance of the UK model should not be over-emphasised. We saw in Section 3 how the Polish and particularly the Hungarian regulatory office framework for

---

[25] See Fingleton et al (1996)

electricity retained considerable intervention powers for Ministries. Indeed, it could well be argued that the Hungarian model is a hybrid with the Continental European model.

The main reasons for adopting the UK office approach seem to be:

- By having a single office head and a small staff, it greatly economises on the resources needed for regulation;
- It fits well with the introduction of competition over networks as required by the EU Electricity and Gas Directives;
- It allows the Government a greater degree of influence eg by the choice of the Head of the Office; and
- It is more able to evolve to meet the needs of changed circumstances than the US or German models.

There are costs to this approach. It can lead to regulatory unpredictability and uncertainty (as US critics argue). But, the attractions of it in CEE countries are clear, particularly given the potential demand for and supply of staff experienced in regulation. In addition, particularly given the pressure from the EU Telecommunications Directives, it is a model that is becoming rather more common in Western Europe.

6. Conclusions

In Stern (1994), I analysed developments in economic regulation in CEE countries in terms of the *demand for* and the *supply of* regulatory services. The argument was that the demand for regulation is related to the need to attract private investment into infrastructure industries like energy and telecoms relative to the desire of the government to retain control over the utilities, while the supply was largely determined by the availability of the specialist human resources needed to operate regulatory institutions (as well as run companies and staff Ministries). However, Stern (1997) suggested that countries with fast growing demand and a secure macro-economic position (like China and the Asian "Tigers" pre-1987) feel much less need for explicit and independent regulation because they are perceived to offer sufficiently good (and secure) market prospects to investors. Hence their governments feel much less need to introduce independent regulatory institutions than countries where there are major investment needs but slower growth or a less secure macro-economic reputation.

These conjectures are useful in considering the lessons from the CEE competition between regulatory models reported in this paper. The two main findings from this paper are:

(i) in those CEE countries which have embarked on serious reform, they have typically chosen, for electricity, to adopt UK-style regulatory offices (albeit with significantly more Ministry involvement than in the UK); and

(ii) there has been little development of independent regulatory institutions for telecommunications in CEE countries, in spite of much higher investment rates and much more liberalisation and privatisation.

The telecommunications experience seems clearly to demonstrate the force of the second conjecture. In almost all CEE countries, there has been major expansion of fixed line systems, substantial investment in one or more mobile networks, considerable privatisation activity and unbundling of incumbent telephone companies, etc. And yet, outside the Baltic States, there is not a single independent telecoms regulator.[26]

The only way of reconciling these facts is that the current and prospective profitability of this rapidly growing industry, plus its general importance for the development of the countries, mean that investors do not feel the need for independent regulatory institutions to protect their sunk investments. In addition, sufficient numbers of high-quality Western strategic investors have bid sufficiently large amounts for franchises for CEE governments not to need to introduce regulatory frameworks with independent regulatory agencies to attract sufficient private investment.

Strong growth in demand and high profitability is palpably not the case for electricity (or gas or water and sewage). The impact of the demand factors identified above is shown most clearly in the Hungarian case, where a first attempt at privatisation of electricity and gas distribution companies in 1993 failed largely because of uncertainties over the regulatory framework, leading to the enactment of the Electricity and Gas Laws. Moreover, perceived weaknesses in the regulatory framework by US and UK companies led to most of the privatisation tenders going to French, German and Belgian companies. The requirement to have a strong regulatory foundation for electricity (and gas) privatisation in these slow-growing markets is again the apparent driving force behind the recent renewal of activity in regulation in the Czech and the Slovak Republics, Bulgaria and Romania.

However, this does not answer why the UK model seems to have emerged as the winner in the CEE regulatory design competition. The answer to that seems to be that it is the way in which some form of independent (or semi-independent) regulation can be set up while economising as far as possible on regulatory resources. The supply factors for regulation have largely determined the style of regulation adopted.

Time and again, the main practical concern in CEE and other countries when establishing new regulatory agencies is the number of people required - particularly high-level staff - and the cost of the agency. There are other contributory factors, notably the ability of Ministries and Governments to maintain an influence on regulatory offices unless the laws establishing them rule this out - and, so far, the main enacted electricity or energy laws have actually or potentially allowed considerable Ministerial powers.

Thus, the evolutionary process has been for Ministries in CEE countries to relinquish their role in economic regulation when the demand for regulation required it (eg because of privatisation or high private investment needs in relatively slow-growing sectors), but

[26] EBRD Transition Report 1998 lists Hungary as having an independent telecoms regulator. My understanding is that the Hungarian Communications Authority has no decision making powers on tariffs; it shares most of its key responsibilities with the Ministry of Transport, Communications and Water Management; it is partially funded from the state budget; and the head of the Authority reports to the Minister of Transport, Communications and Water Management. This seems to me to be just as much a Ministry regulator as the Czech Telecommunications Office which EBRD (rightly) do not classify as an "independent" regulator.

for the style of regulation to allow for considerable future change and a continued Ministerial involvement eg on household prices and the protection of perceived national strategic interests as well as requiring a small regulatory sector. The US model is not consistent with this approach; the German electricity regulation model requires a stronger competition agency than CEE countries have (and this model is anyway not obviously a long-term runner) and the Ministry regulation model does not address the regulatory risk issues faced by investors in CEE electricity industries. Hence, we observe in Hungary and Poland the adoption of small UK-style offices with some Ministry regulation safeguards, a pattern that looks to be followed in the Czech Republic.

These are the proposed explanations for past choices. For the future, the question arises as to whether and how far the new energy regulation offices will become (or be allowed to become) genuinely independent in practice, particularly on tariff regulation. The Hungarian Energy Office has not been allowed to be so. For telecommunications, the question arises as to when the new market arrangements will require a more developed regulatory entity.

In more general terms, it might be expected that EU accession would boost the development of regulatory institutions. However, it is easy to exaggerate the *specific* influences of EU requirements. Regulatory practices in existing EU counties do, however, provide examples of working models to which CEE countries readily refer and on which they draw. This is likely to be enhanced by the "twinning" programme which the EU has recently instituted.

APPENDIX A: REGULATION IN CIS ECONOMIES

It is very difficult to assess the development of regulation in CIS countries. Apart from Russia, they are all new countries having to start almost from scratch in introducing their own political and legal institutions, particularly the set of institutions needed to support private sector, market-based commercial activities. Russia may not be a new country in this sense, but it faces an equally daunting task in devising and implementing an institutional framework suitable for a private enterprise economy.

Some of these countries have introduced regulatory legislation for utilities (eg the Kazakh Law on Natural Monopolies). In addition, the prices and investment of the electricity, telecommunications and other utility service industries are regulated by someone – by a Ministry or a Committee or the President or whoever. Nevertheless, it is difficult to conceive of any of the embryonic new regulatory institutions operating comparably to those in Hungary or Poland, let alone those in Western Europe, North America or Australasia.

The commercial, legal and institutional capabilities in the CIS countries are much weaker. The availability of people to staff such agencies is also very limited and the demand for people with these skills is enormous. Hence, one would expect it to be very hard to sustain independent regulatory institutions. Indeed, the question arises as to whether and how far it makes sense to develop them rather than improved Ministry-based regulation, particularly in the smaller and poorer CIS countries.

These thoughts are partly prompted by statements that are sometimes made about progress in utility and regulatory reform and how some CIS countries are performing. Thus, the 1999 EBRD Transition Report Spring Update classifies the electricity industries of Georgia, Kazakhstan and the Russian Federation along with Hungary as at the highest of 5 stages of reform, defined as:

"Reform progressing radically through unbundling, independent regulator, divestiture and concessions and nascent competition in wholesale supply."

In contrast, Poland (along with the Ukraine) is classified at Stage 4.

In the light of the discussion earlier, the relative rankings of Hungary and Poland may seem debatable. Much weight seems to be given to Hungarian privatisation as wholesale competition is far from "nascent" (MVM has so far resolutely refused Third Party Access (TPA) to its network, which it has the powers to do under the 1994 Electricity Law) and, in practice, Hungarian regulation is, as we showed above, far from independent. Conversely, the Polish government has been far more effective at separating transmission from generation, the Polish Energy Law makes TPA mandatory and the new regulator, at least on paper has far more independence. But, Poland has done little on privatisation and although TPA is mandatory, Hungary appears to be making faster progress in actually implementing proposals for more open access.

The discussion above illustrates the difficulties of making these generalised comparisons. Much depends on the implicit weightings used by the authors. The difficulties grow enormously, however, when the comparisons are made not between countries that are relatively similar in their institutional endowment, commercial sophistication and income per head, but between countries which are very different. Poland and Hungary are very similar on all these factors. Poland (or Hungary) is vastly different on these indicators relative to the Russian Federation let alone Georgia.

This discussion may seem beside the point in a paper devoted to the subject of styles of regulation. That is not so. Comparisons like those in the are not uncommon. Observers are attempting to assess new utility (and other) regulatory institutions on the same basis and criteria as for Central European and OECD countries. But, that seems to me to be a highly doubtful exercise. Given the nature, strength and human capital availability for regulation, it seems unhelpful rather than helpful to lump together for comparison the regulatory structure and style of all CIS countries with those of CEE countries.

This, however, immediately raises the question of whether in 1999, 10 years after the fall of the Berlin Wall, it still makes sense to lump together all these countries as "economies in transition". It may well be that the concept of the single process of "transition" is now increasingly unhelpful rather than helpful, not just in thinking about regulation, but much more widely. That, however, raises much wider and more difficult questions than can be addressed in this paper.

REFERENCES

Cave, M., Stern J., 1998, Regulatory institutions and regulatory policy for economies in transition. In: *Regulating Utilities: Understanding the Issues*. Institute of Economic Affairs/London Business School.

EBRD. 1998. *Transition Report*. European Bank for Reconstruction and Development, London.

Financial Times East European Energy Newsletter 1998-99, various issues.

Fingleton, J., Fox, E., Neven, D., and Seabright, P., 1996. *Competition Policy and the Transformation of Central Europe*. Centre for Economic Policy Research.

Stern, J., 1994. Economic regulation in central and eastern Europe. *Economics of Transition*, September, 391-397.

Stern, J. and Davis, J.R., 1998. Economic Reform of the Electricity Industries of Central and Eastern Europe. *Economics of Transition,* Volume 6 (2), 427-60.

Stern, J. and Holder, S., 1999. Regulatory governance: criteria for assessing the performance of regulatory systems. An application to infrastructure countries in the developing countries of Asia. *Utilities Policy* 8, 33-50.

Stern, J., 1999. 'Utility Reform, Privatisation and Regulation: Lessons from Central and Eastern Europe and from China', *International Business Lawyer*, Vol 27, No 11, December 1999.

INDEX

#

1983 Energy Act, 65
1992 Energy Policy Act, 67
1994 Electricity Law, 125
1996 Telecom Act, 68

A

administrative state, 77
Africa, 116
American market, 21
Amsterdam Treaty, 40, 83
Anglo-Saxon, 53
anti-competitive behaviour, 104
Anti-Trust Authority, 16, 19
antitrust laws, 66
arena coupling, 42
Argentina, 35
ART, 18, 87
Asian "Tigers", 122
ASST, 13, 18
AT&T, 13, 17, 19, 62, 65, 66, 70, 74
Atomic Energy Act, 64
Atomic Energy Commission, 64
Australia, 35, 104
Austria, 39, 40, 105, 112, 115, 116
Autorite de Regulation des Telecommunication, 87

B

Baby Bells, 68
BDI, 39
belief systems, 41, 46
Belgium, 36
Bell system, 74
Board of Gas Commissioners, 62
Bonneville Power Administration, 64
Britain, 4, 5, 12, 13, 15, 16, 17, 18, 20, 21, 22, 23, 25, 28, 29, 35, 44, 48, 50, 54, 55, 58, 60, 61, 62, 64, 65, 69, 70, 72, 76, 77
British, i, 6, 9, 18, 27, 36, 43, 44, 46, 50, 51, 53, 54, 55, 57, 58, 60, 61, 62, 64, 66, 67, 68, 69, 70, 71, 76, 77, 78, 100
British Telecom, 66, 68, 71
British Telecom Act of 1984, 68
BT, 6, 15, 17, 18, 19, 20, 21, 26, 27, 68, 85
Bulgaria, 106, 113, 114, 116, 120, 121, 123
Bundesrat, 45

C

capitalism, 46, 47, 115
CEC, 13, 14, 24
CEE countries, 101, 102, 105, 106, 107, 112, 113, 114, 116, 117, 118, 119, 120, 121, 122, 123, 124, 125
CEGB, 104
Central Electricity Generation Board, 65, 67
Central Europe, 102, 106, 111, 116, 117, 119, 121, 126
centralization, 42, 70, 77
CEZ, 110, 115
Chile, 35
China, 116, 122, 126
CHP, 41, 43
CIS countries, 106, 116, 118, 121, 124, 125
Civil Service, 106, 108
COCOM, 94
combined cycle gas turbine, 35, 73
commercialisation, 110, 116, 120
commodification, 46
common law, 55
communication committee, 93
Communist Party, 101, 121
Communist states, 118
competition, 1, 2, 3, 4, 5, 6, 9, 12, 13, 14, 15, 16 17, 18, 19, 20, 21, 22, 24, 25, 28, 29, 32, 35, 36, 37, 38, 39, 40, 41, 42, 43, 44, 45, 46, 49,

51, 52, 53, 54, 56, 57, 58, 59, 61, 66, 67, 68, 69, 71, 72, 73, 74, 75, 76, 77, 79, 80, 81, 83, 84, 85, 86, 87, 88, 89, 90, 92, 96, 98, 101, 102, 104, 105, 107, 108, 111, 112, 113, 114, 116, 117, 119, 120, 121, 122, 123, 124, 125
Competition Authority, 89, 105
Competition Commission, 103
Competition law, 88
Competition Office, 114
competition principle, 40
competition state, 53, 54, 73, 76
Competition State, i, 51, 53, 54, 72, 76, 77
consumer protection, 40, 89
consumers, 22, 36, 39, 41, 43, 45, 56, 64, 66, 67, 69, 70, 71, 78, 86, 98, 121
Continental Law, 107, 121
Continental model, 121
Contrat du Plan, 104
convergence, 1, 2, 8, 46, 47, 54, 69, 76, 77, 87, 88, 91, 94, 98
corporations, 18, 19, 20, 52, 70
corporatist, 45, 51, 115, 121
CPE, 13, 15
Cross-national policy learning, 21
CSFR, 109, 118
Czech Republic, 102, 106, 107, 109, 110, 111, 112, 113, 115, 121, 124
Czech Telecommunication Office, 112

D

Danmark, 39
de-coupling, 42
Delaware effect, 71
Denmark, 40
Department of Justice, 66
deregulation, 31, 35, 52, 53, 54, 57, 58, 75
DG IV, 3, 19, 38, 89
DGIV, 2, 85, 93, 99
DGT, 13, 23
DGXIII, 93
Digital exchange networks, 74
Direction générale des télécommunications, 13
Director General for Telecommunications, 68
Director General of Telecommunications, 66
disabled, 40
District of Columbia, 62
divergencies, 54, 75, 77
domestic politics, 5, 11, 23, 27
duopoly, 59, 66, 68
duopoly policy, 66

E

EBRD, 102, 110, 119, 123, 125, 126
EC, 1, 2, 3, 4, 5, 6, 9, 11, 12, 13, 14, 15, 16, 18, 19, 20, 21, 22, 23, 24, 25, 28, 36, 48, 83, 84, 88, 91, 99
EC law, 11, 16, 19
EC legislation, 5, 14, 15, 16, 18, 22
EC regulation, 6, 11, 12, 20, 22, 23
ECJ, 2, 79
economic governance, 31, 33, 34
economic growth, 80
economic regulation, 1, 31, 34, 89, 91, 101, 104, 116, 122, 123
EdF, 104, 105, 107
elderly, 40
Electricity Act of 1919, 61
Electricity Act of 1947, 64
Electricity and Gas Laws, 123
Electricity Board, 61
electricity industries, 106, 114, 115, 124, 125
Electricity Lighting Act, 60
electricity reform, 76, 116
electricity regimes, 57, 65, 69, 76
electricity regulation, 46, 102, 124
electricity sector, 4, 38, 39, 67
Electricity Supply Acts, 55
electricity transportation, 73
Energy Act to the Czech Parliament, 110
energy sector, 36, 38, 87, 106, 108, 109, 110
England, 67, 104
entrepreneurship, 63, 64
environmental protection, 4, 37, 40
etatist regimes, 53, 55, 65
EU, i, 2, 7, 8, 9, 11, 19, 25, 26, 27, 31, 32, 34, 36, 37, 38, 39, 40, 41, 42, 43, 45, 46, 47, 48, 68, 76, 79, 81, 84, 85, 86, 88, 89, 90, 91, 92, 93, 94, 95, 96, 97, 98, 99, 101, 102, 104, 105, 106, 107, 109, 110, 112, 114, 116, 122, 124
EU Interconnection Directive, 68
EU regulatory model, 8
European Commission, 7, 36, 38, 45, 46, 48, 79, 80, 85, 88, 91, 92, 93, 95, 98, 99
European Court of Justice, 79
European market, 1, 17
European Parliament, 2, 8, 25, 48, 79, 85, 91, 97
European Regulator, 38
European Regulatory Agency, 90
European Union, i, 9, 27, 29, 31, 47, 49, 72, 79, 80, 98, 99, 100, 101
evolution of regulatory activity, 83

F

FCC, 63, 68, 74
Federal Association of German Industry, 39
Federal Cartel Office, 45, 87, 89, 104, 121
Federal Communications Act of 1934, 63
Federal Communications Commission, 63
Federal Energy Regulatory Commission, 67
Federal Ministry of Economics, 43, 45
Federal Power Act, 63
Federal Power Commission, 63
Federal Regulatory Commission, 81, 86, 89, 96, 97
Federal Trade Commission, 75
Federal Water Power Act, 62
FERC, 67
fixed line services, 112
Florence, 27, 38, 48
foreign capital, 116, 120
foreign investment, 54, 114, 116, 119, 121
France, 4, 5, 6, 12, 13, 15, 16, 17, 18, 19, 20, 21, 22, 25, 26, 27, 28, 35, 38, 42, 44, 48, 81, 87, 107, 112, 115, 116

G

GDP, 116
George Stigler, 51, 53, 75
Georgia, 102, 106, 125
Germany, 3, 4, 5, 6, 7, 12, 13, 15, 16, 17, 18, 19, 20, 21, 22, 25, 26, 28, 29, 35, 38, 39, 40, 41, 42, 50, 87, 89, 104, 112, 115, 116, 121
global change, 53
global networks, 21
goal balancing, 46
Greece, 36, 39, 84
Green Paper, 13, 24
GWh, 36

H

HEO, 106, 107
High level Communication Group, 94
HLCG, 94
Hungarian Energy Office, 106, 124
Hungary, 102, 106, 107, 110, 112, 113, 115, 116, 118, 121, 123, 124, 125
hydroelectric power, 63, 64
hydro-power, 63

I

ICC, 35, 48, 62
IMF, 113, 114
independent regulation, 103, 122
India, 116
institutionalism, 52
interconnection, 4, 14, 16, 25, 54, 58, 62, 68, 74, 75, 112
International Telecom Union, 57
internationalisation, 16, 17, 18, 21
inter-sectoral differences, 34
Interstate Commerce Commission, 62
intervention, 51, 54, 85, 122
interventionism, 77
IPOs, 110
Ireland, 36
Italy, 4, 5, 6, 7, 12, 13, 15, 16, 17, 18, 19, 20, 21, 22, 25, 27, 89, 112
ITU, 57

J

judicial independence, 118
judicial review, 90, 95

K

Kazakh, 117, 124
Kazakhstan, 102, 106, 117, 118, 125
Keynsian Welfare State, 52
Kingsbury commitment, 62
Klaus government, 109

L

Labor Government, 71
labor unions, 65
laissez-faire, 57, 77
Länder, 41, 42, 43, 87, 104
Latin America, 116
Latvia, 110, 113
liberalisation, 1, 2, 3, 4, 5, 6, 8, 12, 13, 14, 15, 16, 17, 18, 19, 20, 22, 23, 79, 80, 81, 84, 87, 98, 102, 105, 106, 110, 111, 115, 116, 119, 122
licences, 14, 25, 88, 106, 107, 108, 111, 113
line-Ministries, 102
Link-Up American program, 70
Littlechild, 44, 46

M

macroeconomics, 52
Mann-Elkins bill, 62
Marxist ideologies, 70
Massachusetts. 62

MED1, 81
member states, 2, 3, 4, 5, 7, 8, 11, 12, 14, 18, 22, 23, 31, 36, 37, 38, 40, 42, 47, 85, 86, 88, 89, 90, 91, 92, 93, 94, 95, 96, 97, 98
Mercury Communications, 66
micro-regimes, 54, 55, 68
Minister of Transport and Communications, 112
models, 1, 5, 8, 33, 67, 87, 101, 102, 103, 107, 113, 116, 120, 122, 124
Monopoly and Mergers Commission, 103
multinationals, 21
municipal socialism, 60
municipalism, 61
MVM, 115, 125

N

National Electric Reliability Council, 64
National Grid, 67
national regulatory reforms, 5
National Telephone Company, 61
nationalization, 62, 64, 65, 67, 69, 70, 72, 73
natural monopoly, 17, 32, 35, 36, 53, 114
negative integration, 42
NCAs, 8, 89
Negotiated Third Party Access, 43
neoliberal agenda, 35
NERC, 64
Netherlands, 40, 60, 112
network-based industries, 35
New Deal, 62
new entry, 65, 104, 116, 119, 120, 121
New York, 3, 5, 23, 24, 25, 26, 27, 29, 47, 48, 50, 59, 62
New Zealand, 35
nomenklatura, 101
NRAE, 113, 114
NRAs, 7, 8, 14, 79, 87, 88, 89, 90, 92, 93, 94, 97, 98
nuclear power, 64, 67

O

OECD, 35, 49, 66, 72, 125
OER, 107, 108, 109
Office of Electricity Commissioners, 61
Office of Electricity Regulation, 67
Office of Energy Regulation, 107
Office of Telecommunications, 18, 66, 87
Oftel, 16, 18, 20, 21, 27, 71
OFTEL, 66, 87, 94, 112
ONP Committee, 93
Open Network Directive, 14
or 'multi-level governance', 23
ordered competition, 4, 53, 57, 67, 68, 73, 75, 76
output targets, 105

P

packet-switching, 73
Paks, 115
pay scales, 106, 108
Philippines, 114
Planning Contract, 104
pluralist, 45, 51, 53
policy frames, 41, 46
Poland, 102, 106, 107, 110, 111, 112, 113, 114, 115, 116, 118, 121, 124, 125
political influence, 21
Polish electricity industry, 107
Polish Energy Law, 108, 111, 125
Portugal, 84
Positive integration, 42
positive state, 51, 53, 77
positivism, 69, 77
Post, Telegraph and Telephone, 13
Postmaster General, 60, 64
Post-Telegraph-Telephony, 56
power plants, 41
prices, 37, 39, 40, 44, 65, 67, 68, 72, 74, 81, 101, 104, 106, 108, 109, 110, 111, 113, 114, 116, 117, 124
Prime Ministerial Ordinance, 108
private investment, 101, 105, 120, 122, 123
private ownership, 4, 6, 36, 56, 57
privatisation, 2, 3, 5, 6, 16, 17, 18, 19, 20, 21, 22, 27, 101, 102, 106, 107, 110, 112, 113, 115, 119, 120, 122, 123, 125
privatization, 31, 32, 36, 39, 44, 52, 54, 65, 66, 67, 68, 71, 75
PTOs, 12, 13, 14, 16, 17, 18, 19, 20, 21, 22, 23
PTT, 13, 14, 18, 19, 25, 56, 87
public hearings, 103, 120
public intervention, 32, 52
public policy, 51
public regulation, 41
public sector restructuring, 23
public service, 3, 4, 40, 41, 43, 46, 62
public services, 2, 53
public utilities, 1
Public Utilities Regulatory Policies Act, 65
Public Utility Holding Company Act, 64

R

railways, 62, 73

rebalancing, 110
RECs, 67
redistribution, 52
reforms, 3, 6, 7, 8, 15, 17, 19, 20, 23, 35, 52, 53, 75, 77, 79, 80, 81, 114, 116
Regional Electricity Companies, 44, 67
regionalism, 57
regulation, 1, 2, 3, 4, 5, 6, 7, 8, 9, 11, 12, 13, 14, 15, 16, 19, 20, 21, 22, 23, 24, 27, 29, 31, 32, 33, 34, 36, 37, 38, 39, 41, 42, 44, 45, 46, 47, 52, 53, 54, 56, 57, 58, 62, 63, 65, 68, 69, 70, 71, 72, 73, 75, 76, 78, 79, 81, 82, 85, 86, 87, 88, 89, 90, 92, 94, 95, 96, 98, 99, 101, 102, 103, 104, 105, 106, 107, 108, 109, 110, 111, 112, 113, 114, 115, 116, 117, 118, 120, 121, 122, 123, 124, 125, 126
regulatory authorities, 3, 4, 7, 14, 18, 40, 79, 86
regulatory capture, 95, 102, 103, 104, 109, 118
regulatory contract, 44
regulatory development, 85
regulatory reform, 1, 2, 4, 5, 6, 8, 28, 52, 88, 112, 117, 121, 125
regulatory regime, 1, 2, 3, 5, 6, 7, 11, 18, 19, 20, 22, 23, 43, 44, 53, 59, 61, 62, 63, 69, 74, 79, 81, 86, 89, 95, 96, 97, 98
regulatory regimes, 3, 4, 5, 6, 7, 8, 32, 41, 46, 47, 57, 67, 69, 70, 72, 76, 81, 85, 88, 96, 97
regulatory state, 2, 26, 31, 34, 51, 52, 53, 76, 77
regulatory structures, 5, 7, 52, 57, 63, 77, 79
renewables, 41
reregulation, 54, 75
re-regulation, 2, 37, 46, 57
Romania, 106, 110, 113, 114, 115, 116, 121, 123
Rural Electricity Administration, 69
Rural Electrification Administration order of 1935, 64
Russia, 117, 124

S

SCEEE, 113, 114
sectoral regime, 45, 54
sectoral restructuring, 37, 38, 44
Securities and Exchange Commission Act, 64
self-regulation, 45, 46
self-regulatory, 39, 44
Slovak government, 116
Slovakia, 121
Slovenia, 117
social market economy, 46
Sprint, 17, 21
Stadtwerke, 43, 104
State Commission for Energy and Energy Efficiency, 113
state institutions, 53, 54, 81
state intervention, 7, 35, 74
state ownership, 21, 61
statist, 65, 116
Stromeinspeisung, 41
structural unbundling, 44
subsidiarity Member States, 79
subsidiarity principle, 38
Supreme Court, 62, 103
Sweden, 36, 41, 44

T

tariff rebalancing, 21
tariffs, 14, 21, 39, 41, 43, 56, 57, 69, 74, 112, 113, 123
tarification, 38
taxing, 51
telecom, 53, 54, 55, 56, 57, 58, 59, 60, 62, 63, 64, 65, 66, 67, 68, 69, 70, 71, 72, 73, 74, 75, 76, 77, 119, 120
Télécom, 4, 17, 18, 19, 20, 21, 26, 27
Telecom Act of 1996, 68
telecommunications, 1, 2, 3, 4, 6, 7, 9, 11, 12, 13, 14, 15, 16, 17, 18, 19, 20, 21, 22, 24, 25, 27, 28, 31, 36, 45, 55, 63, 64, 65, 66, 68, 70, 75, 80, 81, 85, 88, 99, 101, 102, 104, 106, 110, 111, 112, 118, 119, 120, 122, 123, 124
Telecommunications Act of 1992, 112
telecoms, 4, 5, 6, 17, 45, 112, 119, 120, 121, 122, 123
Telegraph Act, 60
Telekom, 4, 17, 18, 19, 20, 21
telephony, 14, 15, 16, 17, 21, 24, 54, 55, 58, 60, 61, 62, 66, 67, 68, 69, 70, 71, 73
Tennessee Valley Authority, 63, 64
terminal equipment, 15, 16, 24, 66
Theodore Vail, 70
Third Party Access, 36
third party access, 37, 39, 113
Third Party Access, 36, 125
Thomas Edison, 59
TPA, 125
trade unions, 3, 4, 5, 8, 16, 19, 20, 23, 44
Transition Economies, 109, 119, 120
transitional protection, 119
transmission networks, 36
transmission system operators, 37, 39
transparent regulatory system, 114
Treaty of Rome, 15
TVA. 64

two-level game, 23

U

UK, 8, 54, 59, 61, 65, 71, 84, 87, 101, 103, 107, 108, 109, 111, 112, 113, 115, 116, 119, 120, 121, 122, 123, 124
Ukraine, 118, 125
umbrella regulation, 113
United Kingdom, 26, 53, 81
United States, 5, 13, 17, 25, 29, 50, 52, 53, 58, 60, 61, 69, 70, 72, 74
United Telephone Company, 60
universal service, 1, 3, 14, 16, 25, 37, 40, 70, 72, 77
Universal Service, 1, 70, 71
US, 3, 8, 9, 17, 21, 23, 31, 32, 52, 54, 57, 59, 60, 62, 65, 66, 67, 70, 71, 74, 77, 99, 101, 103, 107, 109, 110, 111, 113, 114, 120, 121, 122, 123, 124
USAID, 101
USSR, 118
utility regulation, 102, 109, 114
utility sector, 120, 121

V

VDEW, 39
Verbändevereinbarung, 45
vertical system integration, 35
veto players, 43
VIK, 39
vulnerable groups, 4, 37

W

Wales, 67, 104
wayleaves, 61
welfare, 40, 41, 46, 53, 57, 69, 70, 71, 72, 76, 77
Western Union Telegraph, 62
White Paper, 67, 84
Wisconsin, 62
windfall tax, 43
World Bank, 101, 113, 114
World War I. 61